T0268146

CELEBRATING

50 YEARS

Texas A&M University Press
publishing since 1974

I Know About
a Thousand
Things

WITTLIFF COLLECTIONS LITERARY SERIES
Steven L. Davis, General Editor

I Know About
a Thousand
Things

—⟩⟨—

The Writings of Ann Alejandro
of Uvalde, Texas

Edited by
Naomi Shihab Nye and Marion Winik

....

TEXAS A&M UNIVERSITY PRESS
COLLEGE STATION

Unless otherwise indicated, all photographs are from the editors
or are courtesy of the family of Ann Alejandro.

♾ This paper meets the requirements of ANSI/NISO Z39.48-1992
(Permanence of Paper).
Binding materials have been chosen for durability.

Library of Congress Cataloging-in-Publication Data

Names: Alejandro, Ann, 1955-2019, author. | Nye, Naomi Shihab, editor. |
   Winik, Marion, editor.
Title: I know about a thousand things: the writings of Ann Alejandro of
   Uvalde, Texas / edited by Naomi Shihab Nye and Marion Winik.
Other titles: Wittliff Collections literary series.
Description: First edition. | College Station: Texas A&M University Press,
   [2024] | Series: Wittliff Collections literary series
Identifiers: LCCN 2024030935 (print) | LCCN 2024030936 (ebook) | ISBN
   9781648432408 (cloth) | ISBN 9781648432415 (ebook)
Subjects: LCSH: Country life--Texas--Uvalde--Literary collections. | BISAC:
   LITERARY COLLECTIONS / Women Authors | POETRY / Women Authors
   | LCGFT: Creative nonfiction. | Prose poems. | Pastoral poetry. |
   Autobiographical poetry. | Anecdotes.
Classification: LCC PS3551.L3467 I33 2024 (print) | LCC PS3551.L3467
   (ebook) | DDC 811/.54--dc23/eng/20240705
LC record available at https://lccn.loc.gov/2024030935
LC ebook record available at https://lccn.loc.gov/2024030936

Leon she said I am not afraid of snakes or burglars
or sounds in the dark or silence. I am afraid of fire she said
and of fire going out. I am afraid of being swallowed up
not by anything out there she pointed to the canyon
but of being turned inside out and vanishing

—from "Twilight Zone" by Ann Alejandro

For every beast of the forest is mine, the cattle on a
    thousand hills.
I know all the birds of the hills, and all that moves
    in the field is mine.

—Psalm 50:10–11

Please make me famous.
    Love, Ann

(from an email to Naomi and Marion)

Contents

A gallery of images follows page 52.

I Know About
a Thousand
Things

Introduction

Naomi Shihab Nye

"My sister married your boyfriend," she announced loudly, after raising her hand in the classroom full of teachers.

The first words she ever said to me.

Everyone gasped and turned to look at her.

A spunky blonde with pigtails, wearing a checkered red-and-white pinafore-style dress and a devilish grin. I had given my Saturday afternoon in-service educational pep talk about encouraging poetry writing with kids and teenagers, and asked if there were any questions. This was what I got.

"What?"

She sat there grinning, enjoying the spotlight, and shrugged.

It hit me who she must be.

In front of everyone, I said I was happy about the union. It was true! Her sister, the boyfriend, and I had all been friends during college. She kept grinning. I said, "See me later, *ha ha.*" But I felt a little shaken.

Ann would always be an attention-getter, one for a flourish.

In that moment, I could never have known that she would write me thousands of pages for decades and that I would become one of her biggest fans.

⇌

Ann Toombs was born September 30, 1955 in Uvalde, Texas, "the Honey Capitol of the World," a quiet ranching community about an hour and a half west of San Antonio, the same place where actor Matthew McConaughey, Democratic former governor of Texas

1

Dolph Briscoe, Dale Evans, and thousands of other people have been born. Some people outside of Texas may never have heard of Uvalde before the terrible school shooting massacre of May 24, 2022, made everyone hear of it. Ann didn't live to see the disaster, news trucks cramming the town for weeks, flowers piled on shrines, microphones stuck into grieving faces. But she saw so much.

The Uvalde that Ann knew had majestic shade trees, a historic opera house (founded in 1896), a country club, wide streets, numerous Tex-Mex cafes and stores, and an eighteen-hole public golf course along the Leona River. The beautiful public El Progreso Memorial Library was set in a prominent green space in the heart of town. The population was predominantly Mexican-American, as with most smaller towns and cities in South Texas. But Ann's family was white. Her ancestors came to far-flung rural Texas from England and Ireland before the Civil War.

Ann's mother, Gloria Elizabeth Callan Toombs, was an English teacher, and her father, Herbert E. L. Toombs, was a farmer. He raised cantaloupe, cabbage, and onions—round things. He also grew cotton, maize, and other crops. With two older siblings, Liza and Lee, three years between each of them, Ann would grow up to be a fascinating combination of both her parents' interests.

She attended kindergarten and first grade with Miss Ima, who was affiliated with the legendary Uvalde primary school teacher Miss Irene, then made her way through Uvalde public schools. Deeply religious, the family attended St. Mary's Catholic Church when the children were little, then Sacred Heart when the two churches combined. Ann's sister Liza would have a son, Max, who became a Catholic priest, and Ann's own faith would be notable for its deeply rooted conviction and love of Old World ritual.

As children, both sisters went regularly to the library, read a lot, and played outside with friends through steaming Texas summers. They loved going to the rough and rugged family ranch, twenty miles south at Batesville, riding in the back of the pickup truck with scratchy hay bales. Through lingering pink and orange sunsets, they marveled at the vast horizons from the highest hill on the ranch. At home in town, they would drag old Christmas trees into their yards and jump over them like horses.

Ann and Liza were enraptured by their baby dolls in wooden cradles. They took good care of them, bathed and dressed them, and were horrified by girls who did not tend to their own dolls with similar care. They never wanted new baby dolls, only dreamed of new clothes for the old dolls. At age six or seven, Ann submitted some of her writing to a children's magazine along with a contributor's note about riding in the back of the truck. Ann was always writing. "She wanted to express herself and be recognized," says Liza, who now remembers Ann as "a magical thinker." "She gave personalities to numbers, one through ten. She had an imaginary friend named Susie who lived in her big toe. Her imagination was huge."

Ann was always original, and Liza was always interested in her thoughts.

When Ann was eighteen, she married Joe Alejandro of Uvalde, who was nineteen. They had met a year earlier in high school. At that time, an Anglo girl marrying a Mexican-American boy raised eyebrows in small-town Texas. As Joe puts it now, "We had a hidden courtship at first." Their mixed-race romance was more shocking to the community than the fact that they were so young. But their parents accepted it, and they didn't care what people thought. Ann wanted to go to college, and Joe did not, but that didn't stop them. Attending both Southwest Texas Junior College and the Sul Ross University campus in Uvalde, Ann later got a master's in English from the University of Texas at San Antonio. Joe began a career that he still works at today, as a residential home builder and contractor. In his words, he has had a long career in "making other people's dreams come true."

Ann and Joe had two sons, Dylan and Luke, with seven years between them. They all lived on the well-loved property they called Little P ("P" for Pasture) on the edge of town, with a shifting panoply of pets. The more distant family ranch, passed down from Ann's father's ancestors, continued to be their favorite get-away, a sacred gathering place. Everyone in the Toombs-Alejandro gang passionately loved being there. Rushing water, hidden waterfalls, cooling shade, so many scuttling and burrowing creatures, an occasional bobcat—Ann would think of the ranch as her refuge and write about it often.

She taught imaginative English courses at Southwest Texas Junior College, speaking in her distinctive drawl. We had become old-fashioned pen-pals after our first meeting in San Antonio. I was impressed by her passion for books and teaching and accepted an invitation to visit her students. I asked them, "Do you know how lucky you are to have a teacher who cares so much?" She stood in the doorway, debonair, arms crossed. They nodded vigorously.

Later she studied in a summer university program in Chapel Hill, North Carolina, took up weaving at the Southwest School of Art in San Antonio, and, for a time, kept a small apartment in San Antonio. Other seasons she commuted eighty miles each way to make rugs and shawls on her big loom and teach art classes for children. She ran the children's art program at the Southwest School of Art for a while, struggling with the red tape of grants, bulky bureaucratic language, and administrators. She felt deeply conflicted about her love for her small town and ranch land and the opportunities she might have had living full-time in a larger community.

In 1995 Ann published an appealing chapbook of poetry called *Beauty Parlor Poems* through a publisher in North Carolina, though the cover misspelled her first name, adding an "e." She gave a few enthusiastically received readings from this book in Austin, San Antonio, and elsewhere.

Her life bounded along at an ebullient pace, full of relationships and experiences. She became a proud, hands-on grandmother to five granddaughters and one grandson, some of whom lived right next door. Whereas other people made two pies for Thanksgiving, she wrote me that she had made twelve. And she listed them with pride—pumpkin, pecan, buttermilk. . . Her passionate appetite for detail never wavered. I made the mistake of telling her I never liked holidays. For the rest of her life, she tried to inspire me to have a better attitude, describing wrappings, bows, sacred prayers, big meal plans, outfits, and sending me those damn lists of pies.

But her mysterious, debilitating illnesses finally became overwhelming, after first snagging her at the young age of thirty-two. For years she lived and worked in pain, grappling for cures. She roller-coasted through highs and lows. What did she have exactly? After seeing many doctors, specialists, and alternative healers, the diagnosis remained foggy. Fibromyalgia compounded by who knows what other medical complexities? Eventually the illnesses kept her confined to home, bed, and rocking recliner and finally took her life at the age of sixty-four. The pain had wrapped her and Joe up in too many difficult years of unpredictable anguish and diminishing activity. While her deeply rooted faith was shaken, it was never obliterated. It kept her going but also kept her asking why God didn't help her more.

She never stopped hoping, talking, and writing. Through it all, writing continued to spin out of her in manic bursts, first by that staple of life, postal mail, then email, till the end. It is astonishing how many long letters she wrote to her own mother, though they usually lived in the same town.

Somewhere along the way I introduced her to one of my best friends, teacher and writer Marion Winik in Baltimore, who saw and loved in her work what I did—a rambling, generous style, a striking originality, an immense intellect, and an almost crazy-tender love of Uvalde and Texas that continued to nourish her despite all her troubles. Marion had lived in Austin for twenty years herself and appreciated, as I did, the way Ann made the land and world come alive.

There was no one like her. I told people she was the female J. Frank Dobie — with a bit of Elroy Bode's stylistic genius and John Graves's tenderness toward nature mixed in. When I created a Texas anthology of poems and paintings in 2004, *Is This Forever or What?* (Greenwillow/HarperCollins), Ann's piece in the volume was everyone's favorite entry. It is called "I Know a Thinger Two" and is included here.

Ann Alejandro, the best Texas writer almost no one has heard of, died at her home on the rim of Uvalde on June 7, 2019.

Before Ann died, Marion and I promised her we would try to pull a book together from the thousands of pages she left in our keeping. She was very keen on this idea. We tried to get started on it while she was still living but got into such a conflagration over a casually suggested piece of cover art that I knew we had to wait till she died, or the project would never happen. She said she would trust us.

....

Before you settle into this book, you may want to make yourself a bowl of Ann's favorite dish, one that she requested I bring in a huge pot to Uvalde when I visited her during her illness. It can be served cold or hot. No specific quantities were ever offered.

Ann's Favorite

orzo
fresh chives
red bell pepper
tomato
baby spinach
shredded Swiss cheese
olive oil
salt and pepper

Cook the orzo, then add as much of all the other things as you think best.

Advice

This section begins with a piece that was originally published in Naomi's 2004 anthology of Texas poems and paintings, Is This Forever or What? *In many ways, it is the original seed of this book, since Naomi created it by plucking individual lines from the thousands of pages of letters from Ann she already had by then, and, as mentioned in the introduction, it was everyone's favorite piece in the book. Ann was charmed to find that so many of the reviewers mentioned it in their articles. She loved telling what she knew and being acknowledged for her folkloric wisdom.*

We came upon the very last excerpt in this section a few months after the tragedy in Uvalde in 2022. It carried new resonance as we wondered how Ann would have reacted to "the unforgivable" that she mentions here.

❧

I Know a Thinger Two

Coyotes don't care that you are listening.
If your mule loves you and you are standing behind her she
    will cock
one ear back to listen to your voice as she cocks another
    forward to
discern whether there are really turkeys
in the small mesquite stand.
Mules are superstitious.
Sometimes bass bite because they are MAD.
It is very important when you are 6 that your 12-year-old
    brother

bring you back baby snapping turtles
when he skips school
to go to the river.
It is very important to skip school
to go to the river.
It is important to catch grasshoppers, beetles, a praying
    mantis, butterflies,
snakes, lizards, frogs, worms, lightning bugs, and horny
    toads when you are
young, but you need to let them go.
It's good to know exactly where the moon will rise.
Everything always feels out of place until the Big Dipper is
    right side up again.
Everything in a pen wants out during the daytime or the
    nighttime,
depending on its habits.
A family with three small children can sleep soundly in
    their beds for a week
knowing that a six-foot bull snake is loose in their house.
Of course we dream in color.
When you walk or ride the gently sloping hills of Zavala
    County, you know
you are at the bottom of what was very recently a shallow,
    warm ocean.
The whole earth is haunted.
Other people's memories suddenly imprint on our brains.
People who live without streetlights and stop signs and
    maps
aren't as much afraid when there are no
streetlights, stop signs or maps.
A good horse will get you where you want to go
but a good mule will enjoy the view.
Your parents should never make you come inside
just because it's dark or raining.

Every house you see on every lonely road, imagine what you
    would be like
if it had been your home.
The wasp in your hair will probably find its own way out.
Scorpions, tarantulas, and tortoises come out 3 days before
    a rain.
It was better when the milkman came.
Baby birds push the one they don't like out of the nest
no matter how many times you put it back.
When you are raised under a bowl of sky to horizons in
    every direction,
mountains can be terrifying.
Owls will answer you at night.
Buzzards eat live baby lambs.
Cattle and sheep graze all facing the same direction. They
    follow the one
who changes its mind.
Goats love to play king of the mountain, even if the
    mountain is a rusty car or a tree.
A newborn calf stays in its little bed for at least a week
and does not move until its mother calls it.
Donkeys hoard lawn chairs.
Mules don't like anything to change, even your hairdo.
Everything innocent does its part to save the world.
God doesn't love anybody more.
When you talk to mules, they will cock their heads and
    listen to you
before they decide you are not important or interesting.
Half a miracle is noticing. Think of the ones we miss.
Once on a Christmas morning, God gave us a field of
    thousands of white geese.
Sometimes a redbird at the feeder can save your life.
When you live in Southwest Texas, the migrating monarch
    butterflies

orange and gold and lighting on trees, are what God gives
    you instead of fall.
When a spring is gushing from the side of a hill, surrounded
    by
maidenhair fern, and a child asks you, "Where does God
    live?" you say
"God lives right there." And when the spring dries up and
    the hole it made
in the hill is surrounded by dead algae and the river is
    sluggish with scum,
and the child asks, "Where does God live now?"
the answer is, "He lives there still."
To learn where an underground spring feeds into a river,
    you have
to walk the bottom barefoot.

....

If at all possible, don't have only children, because when you are
somewhere between 75 and 90 it will take at least three children, or
preferably more, to keep you alive, and then you have to take into
account the sorry ones who will immediately shove you off to the
nursing home.

Lordy, we shoulda had 8 or 10.

....

Think of the little things that make all the difference. Think of how
on God's green earth somebody had the sense to save Doc's saddle
and pass it on when I was twelve. It is my most treasured possession.

....

I see everything as a river that you just have to jump into . . . become
fully immersed, let it carry you as far as it will, know it. Don't stand
on the banks or wade. Brave the currents and the snakes and the
hazards. It is the only way to know anything—to take it on, to be
active in it.

....

If you love teaching, there is just nothing better to do with your life because it keeps you so dynamic and grateful to be surrounded by so many cute and heroic people. . . . I just love seeing my students everywhere and how their faces light up all over town.

....

You know, I have always thought First Make Peace. Don't set any preconditions for it. Just say, here comes the train of peace. Deal with it. Here are the borders, here are the schools, here are the voting booths, here is the place where each of you is equal, here are the peacekeepers. Here is Amnesty International, here is the Red Cross, the Red Crescent, here are the hospitals and libraries and parks and gardens. Take this. Make peace of this. Make peace in spite of those whose lives are bound up in hatred or conquest or racism.

This is no metaphor.

....

The thing I have learned from fish and love and marriage and children and horses and mules and Saint Anthony is that you never find what you are looking for. You do not find the right fish, the piece of jewelry or wallet lost, the right horse, the right job, the right car or cut of meat at H.E.B. You do not find what it was that God meant three years ago, the perfect place at the river, the color to paint your house, and you cannot even conceive a child till you have ceased struggling. The right things and people always find you when you were not looking at all.

....

Fear is valid and tangible and real. There is some fear you can just avoid . . . like the roller coasters I used to love. Other fears you have to press on—like poetry readings and being on TV and working with the horses—because to avoid them would really diminish your life.

I was active in the brand-new community theater for about 5 years. It terrified me. I loved rehearsal, but I hated performance, though I loved the happiness when it was over. There was only one play which was totally fun for me. I played Stanley, Charlene and Jody in the first-ever "Greater Tuna" played by anyone but the authors. They let us do it because Uvalde was such an outpost, they thought no one would ever find out about it. Instead, we got huge crowds from all over the state and were held over.

....

Good manners are the last word, and eventually see you through everything, because they give nobody any ammunition against you. Good manners are the learned extension of something higher and truer, even if it is not our wish to show good manners, especially to those who have not shown them to us. It is for the time being the closest step we can take to loving our neighbors with full compassion, and it is especially hard for me because when you hurt one of my own I am a mother grizzly bear.

Good manners are the beginning of forgiveness, especially of the unforgivable. If we cannot say to ourselves and mean it, *I forgive them*, then the way to open our hearts is to say *I am willing to try to forgive them*. In this way you can begin some kind of seed of love for people you do not love at all. I don't believe in being fake, but I believe manners can get us through a thousand otherwise hateful moments . . . for example, acts of racism against my husband or children.

I especially hate bad manners in public discourse and politics, and it bothers me a great deal that disagreers are immediately labeled "haters." Moments of love are what carry the human race forward and give us hope and atone for evil by defying the great darkness.

Writing and Mail

In some ways, Ann was the archetypal aspiring writer. She knew she had a gift, but carrying through the administrative duties of getting published and becoming better known were very difficult for her, and this resistance to the grunt work of a writing career was exacerbated by her long chronic illness.

The final piece in this section, "Treasures in the Mail Today," was composed intentionally as a poem, though there's no evidence that she submitted it for publication. In this poem she acknowledges her slowness—it has taken her decades to complete her flatware collection. Heaven knows how long it has been since that "June deadline" she refers to in one of the excerpts that precedes it.

—╱╲—

I think the title of my book should be *Six Hundred Ways to Eat Dirt*, but you know way more about things like this than I do, and I will be helpful and amenable to whatever you want me to think about.

. . . .

Here in Uvalde I had almost always been a big fish in a small pond in English and writing until I got this wonderful PhD English teacher who at first ripped my writing to shreds, gave me Cs, made me cry, humiliated me, and then pared me down to become a much more careful and precise writer. I took eight courses under him. I will always be so grateful to the man who took my raw and self-indulgent talent and sorta turned me into a scholarly writer, a fairly solid literary critic.

But the hard thing about my letters is they are not linear. I can't see the difference between anything. The best English teacher I had said Ann, you are the best student I will ever have, but it's not in you to write paragraphs. I have tried five years to teach you to write a single succinct paragraph.

....

Trust me to forget but somewhere back in the fog I remember a call for submissions with a June deadline.

....

I have a little internet friend, 12 years old, named Will, from Arkansas. He is interested only in hunting, fishing, his potato gun, poisonous creatures, what predators and prey live at my ranch, coons and squirrels. He loves to kill a water moccasin and has many pets, including catfish and turtles. We are wonderful friends. He has wonderful spelling. I was helping him last week with his home-work, and one day we were on adverbs, which didn't interest him a bit. He would type in a sentence and I would try to teach him how to find the adverb. He didn't want that and said to just please tell him what they were, he was tired. So I started doing that, then tell-ing him what words they modified. This went on for four textbook sentences and then he typed in "Will you mail me a tyrantulla?"

....

I am grateful to the 20th century for these things: In any other I would have been not a teacher and writer but a domestic or a butcher's wife or street vendor, illiterate, and half my children would have died. I am grateful for the education I earned at a cheap price at state-supported universities where I had really, really fine teachers. And I am grateful for vaccines and antibiotics and sulfa drugs which helped keep my children alive. I am also very impressed with American plumbing, in which you can count on toilets flushing and hot water at the end of a spigot—I do love a

ready bath and clean eating utensils and trusting I will not get sick
if I drink the water everywhere. I like efficiency and the abundance
of ice and groceries. Other than this . . . I belong with Alexander
Pope in the 18th century.

....

Treasures in the Mail Today

Nine boxes from eBay, catching me up on my life —
A pie plate with a red rim, a pear and apple at the bottom,
A silverplate pitcher from the Rogers company (needs
    polishing)
A set of sweet Baby Bunnykins china,
Bunnies riding a train and shopping at Mr. Pig's general
    store.
A fifties red-and-white tablecloth,
Two footed mugs to match the ones I broke so many years
    ago.

There's a silver tea set on the way,
and loveliest of all, my wedding flatware came.
I'm 30 years late finishing the set people started for me
when I was eighteen. I hold each knife by the handle,
fat, thick, a good weight, beautiful flowing lines and scrolls.
Tiny pickle forks, some kind of unknowable tongs,
things nobody ever uses anymore. I touch them, and say
Finally, you are here where you belong.

Faith

Without a doubt, traditional Christian faith was at the heart of Ann's persona and belief system. Though her faith was challenged by her intense chronic pain and by the realities of life in general, she was always able to reconnect with the spirit through her profound response to beauty in both art and nature. Part of the urge behind her writing is the drive to make sure we feel that too. People! she tells us. You are not on cruise control to Del Rio!

This section also features her capacity for dark humor—both in her reaction to the idea of going toward the light at the time of death, and in her prayers to Saint Anthony regarding people she disapproves of. No stuffy piety here.

⁓⁊⁌⁓

What takes our breath away and fills us with gratitude to have been a part of whatever it is? Where does it come from?

....

The Rules

I have been a Catholic all my life and I know the rules.
Newton knew the rules. Galileo knew the rules.
Einstein, Isaiah, Augustine, Leonardo, Copernicus,
    Magellan, Beckett—
they knew the rules.
Napoleon, Columbus, Ptolemy, Antony, Judas—
They didn't know the rules.
Hamlet, Juliet, Icarus, Faust.,

16

Oedipus, Midas—
They learned the rules.

Animals, vegetables, minerals know the rules.
Stars and planets and moons.
Natural law and order, faith with no choice,
Necessity. The apple falls. Salmon swim upstream.
Three cygnets hatch but only one completes its first
    migration.
The caribou fends off two wolves until they take her calf.
An acorn sprouts. These are the rules.
This is the skeleton. This is the truth.

I failed the trial by fire and I refuse to believe
God wants me to suffer because He loves me. He loves me
and I suffer. One doesn't follow. It is the swallow's broken
    wing.
It is the petal crushed by the broken limb.
The owl intends the mouse no harm.

I thought it was about something else.
Instinctively I arced outward. It was, I thought,
like the universal whorl, about the governing cause
I have always believed to be love. I assumed like any species
we humans operated similarly, but I didn't know the rules.
Once the flight of moths, bats, bees, electrons and sperm
seemed random, whimsical to me. Now words, thoughts,
the things people believe and decide, are
random, disconnected. Freeways are better ordered.

The barnacle clings to the boat. The lichen clings to the tree.
I can only know my own rules.
I cling to the governing cause, I worship the praying
    mantis's

egg case. There is a creek bed that fills me with reverence
and fear.

I want to know what the porpoises know.

I love the mallard that lives in my nephew's water trough.

Surely it is my soul that catches in my lungs for an instant
when the morning sky is wedged with flock of geese.

I ride on the back of the universe.

It bears me by necessity.

....

You really need a confessor who is like a doctor, someone who
knows your history, the history of your evil and your half-struggle
against it. . . I could tell the priest was reading something else, I
could hear him turning pages and I was furious, but then I thought
about all the times I've half-listened to people.

....

About heaven:

Hugs to everybody who can bear it. I stand by a solid steady hug
way more than the vaporous love-n-light people send so often. In
fact, if as I am dying anyone says or telepathizes me to Go To The
Light, I am going to say Fuck you, I'm not going anywhere there's
not a mule. Or I'll choose the place with the juke joint, pulled pork
sandwiches, and ice-cold IBC root beer in brown bottles.

I want heaven to be a very un-diaphanous place where you make
or think of sentences with nouns and strong short verbs and well-
chosen sparse adjectives, like a cottonwood tree on the waterfall
bank of a perfectly clean hard-running Nueces River, beautiful but
familiar as your favorite old shoes and the smell of too-hot cedar
trees, and the smell of sweet earthy whitebrush in a hollow just
cooling off at sunset with the warm air wafting above it, pressing
that basil-lily dusty uncomplicated odor all the way down your
throat and mixing with the smell of your horse or mule's sweat and

how Lee always smelled like a clothesline full of cottons just as the heat had broken.

Cotton gin smells, the mix of old bleached wood and soil and wide indoor boards in the dark interior, polished by the feet and brooms that had crossed them and the oil which had embedded itself into them over decades, a background flavor of machine oil and the sun-dried smell of years of biscuit white cotton that fluffed up like cotton candy and floated up in little clouds all through the dark and light striped air of the gin barn, blown by the huge distant fans or the tiny wisps of low to the ground.

Breezes or the leather of the boots of the men walking by, and the kerosene and dried bean sack smell of the dark brown seeds that permeated the already perfect smell of burlap they used to corset up each dense and heavy bale.

....

My recent prayers to Saint Anthony, my best friend in heaven and patron saint of finding lost things is, "Please St. Anthony, help these assholes find their humility and their just rewards for their evil behavior soon soon soon," and listen, he does it. I think along the lines of boils and herpes, but there have been deaths.

....

When I was little and God was showing me I could sing up the praying mantises and taking me up into heaven so regularly that I saw no boundary between it and earth, He should have told me, Now listen. You are going to feel pain almost beyond the capacity to feel pain. Life is going to beat you nearly to death many many times, and the things that save you will be taken too. This is what is going to happen.

And if He had TOLD me that the wind high up in night that smelt late sycamores wasn't just passing through me, it was me, it was for me, I belonged to it, if He had TOLD me when He opened the veil when I was riding Meg outside the shade of the graves and straight into heaven where I saw Ahma and Boppa and Mommee and Granddaddy Waring and Grandma and Grandpa and Jimmy and all of them going back through time, that they were right there with me all the time, if he had told me then, Look. It is pain and loss from here on out, it must be, I would have said I understand, OK, as I had told him since age 4, I never had to say it in words when I was a child.

....

I think the trajectory of most people's lives is that they grow into and toward God with ever-increasing deepenings of the ancestral voices. And that I was the opposite.

....

All creatures of our God and King! Lift up your voice, then drop dead! Alleluia, oh Praise Him, Alleluia, Alleluia! Oh Praise Him, Alleluia!

....

On beauty:

When I look at something I revere, some wonderful book or song or painting or poem or anything with the spark of God, when I can see that it has the stamp of truth a tree has, or a river, or a hawk circling, I know how profoundly it blesses me. It is like Shakespeare said—there is an art that we create that is the same as nature, us making it in the same way God made the universe.

This dance was finer than a tree or a star or a play or a painting or a symphony, and it opened my eyes to a beauty I never knew was there. My response was one of anguish to see a beauty I have not yet lived, will not live until I die and become one in the round of angels. It was like seeing a glimpse of heaven, the best part of heaven, and then having to come back down and live out your life. It was a thing to remember and aspire to and hope for and want harder than I have ever wanted anything. Imagine that a man could evoke that in a dance. Imagine the love; imagine the piece of God in him, to be able to conjure that wizardry.

....

I always want the choir to remember the gorgeousness of the songs they've been singing for a hundred years. I don't want them to take the beauty of those songs for granted. I want to remind them they are not on cruise control to Del Rio.

....

This morning Joe called me early out to the cold front porch. We could hear thousands and thousands of sandhill cranes across the river in their early-morning honking rites, preparing for their day. I say to God over and over again, "For me? For me!" This sweet earth is as faithful as God, it is his voice and his arms and his smells and all that he made because he loved so much. When I look at it and think of him, I am ashamed of myself for being not half so faithful or brave as an iris bulb. He can count on an iris bulb. He can't count nearly so much on me.

....

Say your prayers. In all things, rejoice and thank God. You told Him, from the time you were four, that you didn't want to miss anything. Well, that's a child's prayer answered.

Land

For Ann, the land was everything, and some her strongest work was nature writing. The connection with the earth she formed as very small child was the heart of her faith, which really was a kind of Christian pantheism. She could never understand why everyone couldn't see and feel what she did—what was wrong with these city folk? As much as she was attracted to museums and high culture, the land had a gravity, a physical pull, that always drew her toward the horizon. This is something that Ann shared with her fellow Uvaldeans, an intense pride in their scrubby terrain; Matthew McConaughey's memoir Greenlights *expresses it fervently as well. "Hearty people formed by this hard land."*

━ʌ━

In March the bluebonnets will be glorious so you must must must come, but in snake boots because they emerge furious and snapping in teeming hordes from dens on exactly March 6. We can roast marshmallows and listen to the multitudinous bands of coyotes and . . . we will have no armor, we will await the purpose of the day and though we nearly miss it, the purpose of all days is Watch, Listen, Learn.

. . . .

I will be so glad if you get to come this spring. In addition to the donkeys, you will be greeted by more than fifty exotic chickens with Tina Turner hairdos, a fresh crop of kittens, two darling big old yearling calves, the parakeet, finches, gerbils, dogs, and now a growing group of fat triangle-shaped field mice whom we catch and put in a gerbil cage.

from Getting There from Here:

I want to tell you about these roads
that bisected my life with bridges over rivers
I had known. Latitude and longitude converge
upon the point where I lived until the roads
became my limbs and the rivers my veins.
This one, southwesterly, returned me to my river
eyeball to eyeball with the fat coyote—I saw
the Mexican eagles, and in the flood
the javelinas and turkeys scrambling
for higher ground. It is a myth about how creatures
won't look you in the eye. They will. Still
I wanted to get on with it, cross the border
where the palomas tristes mourned outside of surgery
and fat unshorn sheep grazed in a vacant lot.
Still there were bluebonnets
and in the grey, cold days sandhill cranes
dropping to furrowed rows where seeds waited.
I lie on a rock by the river
listening to the water run on, and I wonder how long
it takes to get to the bridge from where I cannot
see. I watch two lazy buzzards ride their current
against the green and the bluffs and I know
they have not come for me. Night comes
and here around me is earth water wind and fire
I breathe deeply to make me strong.
They tell me to walk an hour a day
And because I live in the center
of the roads that flare out like
spokes and because I traverse them
all to ride the wheel, I know the
way you go to get well gives you as much
as what they give you when you get there.

....

Fly-fishing is a religion I recognize, and believe in, and approve of—
the supernatural world just caressing you, enveloping you, treating
you so tenderly when it snows, when the brave crocuses come up,
when the house finches come to the feeder, when the flocks of
sandhill cranes fly over you with their trill, when something is so
beautiful, so perfect, so holy you can hardly stand it.

....

Two months late, and after two weeks of inability to get going, I
planted 52 flats of seeds today. Major triumph. This is like my sav-
ings fund, which does not exist. I plant so I will be able to go out
in the yard and get myself saved, knowing the flowers and veggies
and strange, wonderful vines will save me. I sowed in the spring
so in the summer I would be recalled to life. It will be proof to me:
yes, you wanted to live.

....

I planted half the garden today. It means I will live at least until fall.
It is the life I invest now so in summer which will be so awful with
no rain, I will remember who I was, that I had hope, that I loved
life, wanted to love, wanted to see myself in months ahead for the
times when I will have vanished which is most of the time now.

....

I weave and with my hands I try to make small beautiful things,
and I love the ancient rhythms of back and forth and forward and
back. I love the cotton that somebody grew and the wool that came
off some sheep's back.

....

My yard thinks it's in heaven. I have gorgeous banana and big green
lovely bell peppers, and the fall tomatoes are growing up nicely and
the spring tomatoes are setting again! Lordy, it almost makes you
wish it would never freeze. I have me a winter garden growing here
from the remnants of the spring garden that survived that awful
summer and now has this zest for life I find miraculous.

I have been thanking God so much. How He made up to us all in one month the anguish of two nearly unbearable springs and summers. How every thunderclap said, "See, I did not forget you," to everything, every goat and lamb and cow and deer and bird and horned toad and tree and bush and crop, and all of us who live here and endured those two years. It is just the nature of this nature. You have to store up what will not come again maybe for years and be strong enough to survive on what you stored—what the earth and the pockets and the dirt and the springs stored for you. We love rain better than what most people does. We love rain more than people in Louisiana does, I reckon.

....

I think my children will always love the river. Town can never teach you the peril of beauty and the preciousness of its very will to be; it can never shape you to immerse yourself in that kind of redemptive solace. I wish I could teach them to love the ranch, where the chance of bad encounters with humans is so much lessened, but its river is haunted and spooky, and it is desperately hot and harsh, and I did not love it either until I was much older than they are.

....

The sweetest of all smells draws in as evening cools down the earth, the whitebrush like a bridal path smelling of lilies and dust. The hard country that supports an infinite variety of life. Kissing each bluegill or bass on the fly rod, stopping to let the mule & dogs sniff the mystery of the box tortoise, braking for the tiniest horny toads and moving them off the road, the baby pink javelinas who would nurse off any mama or auntie, and their big brothers or cousins snapping at them saying NO this corn is mine! The haunted Leona River and great gift of the Nueces flowing like God's own glory through a desert where no river had the courage & might to do.

Sneaking out the window as a very small child to hear the wind in the trees and the utter silence, going to say hello to each neighborhood dog, climbing the tallest sycamores to let the wind rock me. Then slipping back in my window content that the night had held me in safety. . . . I loved the world too much. I couldn't help it. How could I not? This was the place a mighty and tender God had chosen for me. How could I not see his greatness his safety his beauty in all of it?

....

It was not the thinkers and philosophers who wanted to subdue and conquer the West . . . it was pretty easy for them to see God in nature when they didn't have to hack trails through it, face angry grizzly mother bears, endure blizzards and droughts, killing something for every meal or starve—they didn't have to get bitten by rattlesnakes and swarms of flies. The West, the horizon, was an idea for them. The actual tamers and settlers were the people with blisters on their feet who wanted prosperity, something they could call their own—the actual westering movement was not a movement of the wealthy or educated. It was poor people who saw opportunity and took great risks to have what might be had.

Also it is important to remember that the "wilderness" was not virgin as they all called it. It was not without mythos, it had its sacred places, landmarks in the oral traditions and folklore and religion of countless Indian tribes and Spanish-mestizo descendants . . . the English-speakers renamed valleys and rock formations and canyons and mountains and rivers that already had names. I am amazed at how Whitman and Emerson could be so ecstatic and optimistic when Winfields Scott was marching the Cherokees off on the Trail of Tears. At least Whitman got his hands dirty, grieved, worked through the tragedies. Emerson was large in thought but insular in experience. It was a neat world, there, Concord.

Poe looked inside and saw chaos at the heart of the human psyche. He was 50 years ahead of his time, should have been roommates with Henry James. I resent it that the explorers and writers and settlers and painters felt so unburdened by a past in the land which awed and drew them. It had a past. It just wasn't their past. It had a story, a religion, a history, a mythology. It just wasn't *theirs*.

....

Uvalde to Brackettville in September—

The land forgot it was the end of summer
and looked like April, spread before me
a banquet of the spring that didn't end.
A hard land for hearty people
has few mercies and no memory
But I store its treasures up
to sustain me . . . thick grass . . .
guajillos uncurling . . . blooming cenizos. . .

I am of hearty people formed by this hard land
that's soft and nourishing now
a band of unhardened survivors. . .

Some land, I know, is always home.
It claims you. And the people
who see it in your bones—
the way you carry yourself
the way you stoop and smile and almost cry.
the way your eyes scan the sky and know what it means—
they take you in. They dust you off.
They spread out the banquet.

It's America, right. What can happen.

Snakes

If Ann had written a book-length memoir, this gives a sense of what it might have been like. Ten thousand pages like this!

⇀ʌ↼

I really have no objection to snakes. I was only ever scared of one when a gorgeous fresh skinned Texas rat snake landed on my arm. It had fallen from a huge palm tree where it had been looking for oriole babies. I was watering my gourds with the hose and it landed on my arm. I had to pluck it off, with my other arm—both of us quite startled—and toss it into my gourd jungle.

For all the people who hate snakes, please realize that without them our temperate planet would be overrun with rats, mice, moles, and voles. Even the poisonous ones do us a huge service.

However there is nothing so revolting and odious to me as seeing hundreds or thousands of snakes at the same time emerging from their dens. I almost retch. Even the three rattlesnake heads and necks which popped out simultaneously from a caliche hole the size of a half dollar unnerved me like Aww man that's a hideous close call and subsequently I named the place "Rattlesnake Jump Out and Bite You Hill" and never took the dogs there again.

I don't know if it's an old wives' tale or not but we throw the heads high into the tallest guajillo brush and hang the bodies on fences; I guess this is our way of feeding the critters, but I think it's part voodoo too.

I prefer my snake encounters one by one. Joe hit a trifecta the other day, a rattlesnake basking, a Texas bull snake the length of the width of the road, and a coachwhip standing at its fullest possible height all on the same road by the river.

One night Lee's very large, angry and hissing (rat) bull snake used all his strength to just bust open his cage door and remained at large in our house for 6 days. As we lived, cooked, vacuumed, ate, washed dishes, got clothes and shoes out of our closets and slept in our beds… Mama was sitting in her rocking chair in the living room one day and looked at her mother's cherry buffet in our tiny house and realized, "That's got to be where it is," got a flashlight and—sure nuff—when Papa got home from the farm, he got a gunny sack (weren't gunny sacks wonderful and don't we miss them?), reached for the upset hissing snake's neck, pulled him out, plopped him into the sack, and knotted it.

When Lee got back from school, Papa handed him the sack and said, "Take this back to the ranch." He wasn't mad or anything, he just knew what boys do and wanted the snake back to its rat killing. Nobody was mad or scared, though as a six-year-old opening my dark closet I always listened very closely before I went in and watched (closets didn't have light bulbs in that era) where I stepped. Before I went to bed I rubbed my arms all over the mattress, under the pillow and between the sheets, and looked under the bed with a flashlight. I wouldn't stand barefoot at the kitchen stove knowing they always go to dark warmth, and since I was at school I missed Papa's stick-your-hand-in capture.

Papa was pretty invincible, he had brought down a Focke-Wulf in the war. He won every pigeon or skeet shoot he entered, he fished me out of an ice-cold Leona River, as a child he had a skiff where he fished the Houston ship channel, he was a boat boy, caught a sailfish (they can pierce your brain) and rays by accident, marlins, barracudas, tarpons, lots of snakes for me. He cut the barbed wire fence where a furious javelina with huge tusks was scared and mad as hell to let it free. I really thought there was nothing my father couldn't do including picking up five-year-old me and handing me to a boat manned by Mexican shrimpers so I might have the thrill of riding a sea turtle's back while a swimmer from the other boat swam alongside me.

How many people get to say that as a child they rode on a sea turtle's back until it was ready to submerge? I then slid off, and the fisherman handed me back up to Papa on his friend's boat. Papa of course gave everyone in that crew some kingfish and redfish, and a sixpack of ice-cold beer. He asked me, "How did that feel?" and I said, "It felt real strong!"

Animal Kingdom

Obsession is not too strong a word to describe Ann's relationship with animals, from her beloved mule Chess Pie to mules in general, to her many generations of dogs, to the monarch butterflies migrating through her ranch each year. We mentioned our debates with her about the packaging of this book—here she tells us that she wants her mule in her author portrait. Because of her great love for dogs and respect for snakes, the story of what happened to her little dog Frankie is particularly poignant.

When Ann gets to heaven she'll know it—Louis Armstrong will be playing, and she will get to stroke the velvety nose of the great Secretariat.

—ı₁—

I can't tell you the times my mother took me down to those pens in 45-degree sleet after school or on weekends said, "I'll pick you up just before dark unless you want to come home early and if you do, just ride her in," and on those cold days I rode bareback in a fleece cap because bareback was so much warmer. I was 11 or 12 years old, by myself on 250 acres, or on Hacienda Road. Louis Capt would drive by every single day and see me riding in the sleet or heat, and honk or wave, when he was going to check on the progress of his corn plants.

In the pasture I would turn around backwards in the summer tall grass, with no bridle or halter, and rest my head on Blondie's ample butt and let her graze as I slept or read a book. When she figured it was time for evening oats, she would just walk back to the pens with me still lying down striding her backwards.

I would walk in sweaty and dirty scratched and bloodied and my mother would look up from a book and ask, "What did you do today?" Gulping water straight from the tap and I said, "I herded Spanish goats on somebody's ranch." "Oh, sounds like fun."

From the moment he first let me ride barely three-year-old Blondie, gentle but just as green as I was, I knew I could never recover from my adoration of her. Marna came out and met and loved him and his sweet wife who wore her silver white hair in Amish-style braids. Mama said he told her, "There ain't no two better matched. Them two was made for each other."

He looked at Mama guiltily when she asked if he'd sell her and said, "I'd have to charge you four hunnerd dollars. I couldn't let her go for less," and my guts were twisting in my lungs. That was more than Mama brought home in a month of teaching 8th grade. Then Mama brilliantly but almost fearfully asked, "Would you consider letting me pay her out at a hundred a month?" and he said, "Oh sure, I could do that just to see how happy she makes that little girl. Just look at em. They even look alike."

School was just a constant itch. I would look out the windows toward the pasture and at 3:30 trot home as quick as I could to put on my jeans and boots so the minute Mama got off work at 4 from the same school she could drive me out to that pasture where Blondie swished her yellow tail and slowly walked up to me, smelling my pockets for cookies.

....

I was good with cattle. I knew how to tame them and herd and pen them and load them and settle them down and keep them from running off. And I would like to do that again. I saw on CBS cattle prices were 15 cents a pound. It broke my heart. Heartland = hard land.

....

Okay to the photograph, but I truly think Michael's lens cannot find me unless he meets my darling mule, Chess Pie. The way her face looks into my face. Chess Pie and I go to a world without words; at sunset there is a rounding road on a hill from which we can see not a sign of any human at all, only the bowl of sky equaled to the earth around us. We can see southwest to the clouds forming on the Gulf of Mexico that will bring us the wind in the evening; we look north and we can see the Uvalde water towers, Mount Inge, the hills at Knippa, and the hills of all three rivers which spill into the valleys—the Nueces, the Frio, and the Sabinal.

....

Don't send me anything anymore unless it's real shallow or about guns. Luke took me shooting and we found that I was quite good at it. I reckon I could kill a rattlesnake no regrets, but would definitely hide from a feral hog. Luke calls them up with his own piggy sounds, then blasts the shit out of them, which they require.

Sr. Francis Joe strikes again. When he went to the ranch between football games to feed ravenous horses, mule and the cattle that aren't even ours, he found this little weak freshborn calf bawling meekly, lying across the fence from his mother. Joe hoisted him over to his mother who began licking his umbilical cord. Darling calf was really confused and disoriented but did stand up to begin suckling on his Mama. Joe stayed with them until he was sure she had accepted the baby. Brave good cow Mama. Brave good calf saver Joe. It is thundering and there are huge great orange cells all around us but it has happened so many times over the last two months I hardly dare mention it much less pin any hopes on it.

....

Early today KPAC was playing the theme from "Lawrence of Arabia" and I took it as a real good sign. Those Arabian horses are the ultimate in strength, gentleness, sweetness, intelligence, endurance, trainability. They've certainly always been my favorites in their looks. They're the most beautiful of all.

....

I think it should be illegal to raise horses in stables. They need to know what life is like outside and not be so scared of idiot things like bushes.

....

On the old Eagle Pass Road, Joe saw three bears at night, yes. He turned the car around. It was three bears, one smaller than the other two. Everyone but Goldilocks on the highway. Yes, it's true. Joe and I saw an ocelot hiding near a culvert on the same road, after a flood, when we were on our way to Mexico.

....

My mornings are watching the painted buntings, lover by lover, playing in the iron, rusty plough disk that Lee turned into a bird-bath years ago. The cardinals and hummingbirds are constantly at the feeders, and a sweet whispery wind catches at my hair. The low guajillo hills are green and beautiful, and I never turn on the air conditioner. Yesterday a box tortoise came to visit.

....

I have been on a quest for monarchs. There aren't as many this year. Last Friday, Liza and I went to the ranch, riding from motte to motte, to riverbed to riverbed—and saw a pretty great number in the big motte. Then on our way out, the river crossing was absolutely filled with them. They are what God gives Texas instead of fall.

The next afternoon I went with Joe. We rode to the little waterfall grove where my aunt and grandparents are buried, then through the waterfall motte, and back to the pens. The sunset, and then high in the sky fluttering above us were groups of monarchs, all heading toward another tiny oak motte. I yelled at Joe, "They're in this one!" We walked down into it and were utterly surrounded by this thousand-fold fluttering of orange and black glory. We just sat there in the twilight, listening. It was so quiet you could hear their wings meeting at the top when they came to rest on a branch.

How does something so weightless travel so far?

....

I have always found comfort in the consort of birds, the hide and flight, the fuss and fume, the beak-biting and nest-building.

I have been in love with birds since the most painful time in high school of my growing up. I truly live by birds. They are so beautiful, so perfect at what they do, and able to fly away. My life has been saved by the birds at my kitchen window feeder. All the gorgeous cardinals that stay year-round, the finches and orioles and painted buntings, and this year a flock of green jays. The sandhill cranes migrating. And geese, as a matter of fact.

This Catholic has become a pantheist.

....

Well you know, I'm a romantic. Always falling in love with SOMETHING. Now it's orangutans, elephants, lions, tigers, pangolins, cheetahs, bison, wild mustangs, and burros. But mostly elephants and orangutans. They're the most likely to be extinct in 20 years or all in sanctuaries and zoos.

....

What a tale I have to tell! About how Poolie collapsed on our ride this weekend, and literally fell and rolled as if she were dead—limp, then stiff, eyes glazed, pupils enlarged, and complete dirty-tongue stillness. I gave her mouth-to-mouth resuscitation nothing. Then I tried it again, and she started gasping in these huge, choking irregular breaths, and I thought she was still going to die, but at least she could hear me and know she was with me. But then her breathing got better and better and her eyes came back into focus, and Joe raced her on Little Boy down to the river to cool her off. He bathed and patted and dripped water over her and she revived.

....

Just after sunset tonight at the ranch after a good ride with Lee, my little dog Frankie was bitten by a rattlesnake. I was holding him close to me when he died. He was so shocked when he yelped and ran to me, like "What on earth happened to me?" No one took more joy out of the ranch than Frankie or was more energetic and happy chasing rabbits, or obedient about staying very close to us.

It got him in a whitebrush thicket as he was running by. We never saw it. We were only 5 minutes from the end of the ride and on a road for the first time the whole evening.

I don't know where to sit. I don't know where to sleep. I don't know how to do anything without him curled around me somehow. My shirt, my chaps, my boots are covered in his poor snake-bitten blood. Poor Joe, that weary task of burying things we love.

....

If I get to heaven I want to be met by Louis Armstrong & Secretariat. I want to hear Louie sing "What a Wonderful World" and "Hellzapoppin." And I want to stroke Secretariat's nose. I don't want to ride him. I just want him to honor me with his company.

I keep thinking my God if I die, I don't want anybody to know how many SHOES I had or how much fabric I left unsewn not to mention all these clothes. Today I crawled up to the bed and prayed to die but was awakened by a chihuahua. I prayed for God to bring me home and he let a chihuahua in. I had closed the door too. You want to be greeted by Louis Armstrong and all your kin and instead it's this hot earth and a chihuahua.

Circle of Stars

Ann was particularly proud of this meditative essay, several versions and copies and copies of which turned up in our files. "Circle of Stars" was her title; she may have written it for a writing class she took.

—⁾⁾\⸝—

Six lawn chairs stand in a circle where we left them last night after we sat in them for hours, looking up at the August meteor showers and showing each other Scorpio and Taurus. This morning in the full sun with heat already rising from the packed dirt in this yard, they look like they did something secret without us after we finally wandered off one by one into the darkness and slept. Somebody will drag them to various points of shade all day long, and tonight again, one by one, they'll be pulled back into a circle, and somebody will start telling a story that will remind somebody else of another one to tell, and two or three will make plans for tomorrow or the next day, and the children will wander up when they can't see their marbles or water guns anymore, and ask us what we mean by the tag ends of what they hear.

Deer will snort in the field, and an owl will lift himself out of the leafy clumps of one of the oak trees we're under, silent as nothing, kill something sixty yards away, then disappear against the black slur of hills that surround us. There are wild boars in the hills, and sometimes cougars, and caves bats leave in the evenings. There are springs that feed into the river from cliffs the river cut from the hills thousands of years ago, and maidenhair fern sprouts where the water drips from limestone walls.

I think those chairs told stories about us last night when some of us were asleep in beds and the headlights of the rest of us were long down the highway shining in the eyes of deer and raccoons, rolling sixty miles an hour down the hills toward home. Those chairs or the wind or the moonlight that came and filled them up.

I caught a little fish yesterday on my nephew's reel for the first time in many years. We were sitting on the roots of bald cypress trees and casting into the shade. My hands remembered the spiny top fin, the slippery body, as I worked the hook out of the fish's cheek. I talked to him about being foolish and how next time he would know better, and when the hook was free, dropped him into the river. I smelled my hand and I didn't want to wash the fish off. Now I think our stories have crossed in some unresolved subplot, or maybe I have been the informing event of his youth, his bildungsroman, and he will live to warn his grandchildren, show them the scar on his lip.

I look up into these hills covered with trees except for the ridges of sheer rocks where caves open, and I know they have secrets. I see the red-tailed hawk gliding along the cliffs by the river, and I know he has a home. The grey fox that stares at me, her kit who runs across the gravel road have a home here somewhere, a place where they meet and rest and watch.

I always felt like the hills and the trees, the dry creek bed and the river, the springs and the caves knew something separate from me, held collaborative memories with patience and dignity, something between the root and the bedrock it cleaves, *Oh, it's you.* They give each other permission. They give permission for me. And when I see the circle of chairs, I wonder if the stories came from us and we told of the hills, the constellations, the bats, the wind, and the cone of moon, or if the stories were already there and told to us before anyone ever spoke. I am at the end of something, and at the end of something people still look for signs. I know I could be a hill, quietly bearing my own weight and past and future. A hill never reinvents itself. The rocks just fall and the floods just come and the sun just bears down hard.

The ocean just left these hills millions of years ago. Nothing violent made them. They have soft ridges. Wherever I have been, I measure places against them, and whenever I come back, something tight in my shoulders lets down as soon as I see them from the window of a car or airplane. I don't live in these hills; I never have. I just come to them every once in awhile. But from the time I was very young, I thought of them as my home. You can see them, north and lavender, from my balcony. I don't even mind the mid-afternoon heat or the blurry whine of grasshoppers as big as my thumb.

All my life heat has smelled like the junipers we call cedars that grow here. I like to chew on their foliage that isn't leaves. I like to bite into the red center of their branches. I like a cedar stick to peel, and a cedar Christmas tree. I'm lucky not to have allergies; cedar is terrible for people who do. I'm not allergic to anything. Everyone who walked with us through the creek bed three days ago came out infested with chiggers, except for my brother and sister and me.

You have to stretch so large to contain this land that you can look a hill through its center and say, I know you, you old solid rock with vein of springs and caves and a skin of grass and trees where animals live. One by one, those dreams of my one-by-one losses stop. Two days ago I dreamed I was surrounded by seven-year-olds reading to me. The pang of it was as fresh as any of the old dreams ever were, because two weeks ago my sister, husband, son, and I packed up the most recent of the many classrooms where I have spent most of the last fifteen years of my life, and hauled it away, probably for the last time. My dreams of little children loving the heroes of the Trojan war will dwindle, too, and stop.

But I have always dreamed of rivers, treacherous and beautiful with labyrinths under waterfalls and rainbows in the spray, upstream journeys with children and my sister, arduous passages, slippery banks, tangled foliage, children falling in, always children saved, always the journey to the source of the river and never arriving and urgency to round the next bend and scale the next waterfall. In my river dreams I am valiant and strong. Not a single one is lost. We always make it to the end of the dream.

I try not to look back. I try to cut my losses as if they were fish I thanked, released and wished well, or to stand up like Clint Eastwood at the end of a movie, get on my horse and press on. But the dreams, for a while, look back. I used to dream of my horses, too. l think dreams make you brave.

Now I don't know what I am for, and I look to these hills and the circle of stars to tell me, and I think I am just one of their stories. Sometimes Taurus up in the sky glares down on me accusingly, as if I ought to know more than I do. I think he is a fine, mean Greek bull and that I ought to be able to offer him something he isn't tired of knowing and seeing.

There is a creek bed here that is like *Journey to the Center of the Earth*. You start out at the windmill, the Papalote for which this place is named, and you walk down and down limestone steps and geometric floors like the rooms of Roman houses. When it rains, the water from the hills pounds through the bed with sudden violence on its way to the river, and then it's almost dry again in a few minutes. These are flash floods that change the creek bed every year and wash down new artifacts from the geological history of this place. In the flood of a Cretaceous upheaval, the seabed covered and drowned a huge vein of what lived there, and walking today you can find and dig out fossilized clams, snails, oysters, and all kinds of little prehistoric creatures with hundreds of legs. They look like African masks.

Sometimes a hawk flies over you, or you can hear a javelina grinding its teeth because it smells you and wants you to go away.

A long time ago in the dim twilight, standing in the bed underneath the horizon, I found an object so strange I had to poke it with a stick before I would touch it, because it looked alive, like the coils of the monster in *Alien*, or one of those huge misshapen fungi that grow at the roots of oak trees, something for witches and trolls. It had the face of an elephant, with a long trunk and two ripped ears. It rang against my stick, hard as rock, and then I saw what it really was—three stalactites grown together, snapped in half down the middle, a cross-section, washed down from some cave that probably collapsed on itself in prehistoric years. You can touch the ridges where the lime from the water deposited itself year after year, dripping from the roof of the cave. It's the best thing I ever found. I think I was well when I found it.

I gave it to my parents. We call it the elephant rock, and they took it to the coffee table of their house at the ranch, where it sits by bowls of arrowheads, spear points, and hide scrapers. Everyone who sees it is a little afraid at first, just like I was, and they want to know its story. "Where did you get that rock? It looks just like an elephant." Now I have brought my parents, my brother and sister and their children to this place and this creek bed. I am almost afraid to over-praise it, especially to my own family, so when I said, "It's the most wonderful place you've ever been; it's like going back in time, and it's sort of haunted, it's where I found the elephant rock," I thought I probably should have said less. If they came and thought, big deal, it's a creek bed, I would have felt embarrassed and stupid. But they love it, too, and return to it.

My father digs out perfect shells of clams, my sister came away with that water-bug with all those legs, and my brother made us follow it all the way to the river. Our eyes are always looking down for something wonderful. At intervals, the bed falls off in four- or six-foot ledges, and you have to hold onto the sides of the bank to creep down the narrow slopes or steps of rocks, unless you are the children, who jump. I stepped down our path the other day and pulled my foot back up to look at the rock I had stepped on. It was wedged in the ground and covered with dry silt, but I knew its shape—another elephant rock, three stalactites, joined at the sides and split in half, cross-sectioned down the middle. Finding it felt like fate, twice in ten years and a few blue moons.

I brought the rock to my parents, who will take it to the ranch to sit beside the other. I like to believe they are twins, or even better, two halves of the same broken one. I want to be what joined them after who knows how many ages or what stories separated them. I think they will not have to tell each other. Oh, they'll know. *It's you.*

An Interview

We were charmed to find this 2005 e-mail interview conducted by Ann's niece Camille in her papers. By the way, the "hateful little mean white town" was Uvalde, which she never forgave for its reaction to her early marriage to Joe Alejandro, which at the time was frowned upon by people on both sides of the racial divide.

—◢◣—

What is your full name and birthday?

Ann Toombs Alejandro 9/30/55
That is all you are getting from me

What are you wearing?

Blue and yellow waffle, that is called Seersucker

What was the last thing you ate?

Cooked eggs and mushrooms and cheese at 11:30 last night

What are you listening to right now?

Trashy TV

Do you wish on stars?

Yes

If you were a crayon, what color would you be?

Cornflower blue

How is the weather right now?

Humid and hot

Last person you spoke to on the phone?

A lying car saleswoman

Do you like the person who sent this to you?

OF COURSE!

How old are you today?

49

Favorite drink?

HEB generic diet orange

Favorite sports?

Pillsbury bake-off

Favorite month?

January, it's long and cold and fires at night and no yard work

Favorite foods?

Enchiladas
Chili dogs
Frito pies

Favorite day of the year?

Christmas Eve

What do you do to vent anger?

Whine, write, call Liza, cut off my hair, take 60 pills, and/or burn myself with cigarettes

What was your favorite toy as a child?

Madame Alexander Kitten doll

Summer or winter?

Winter—fires in the fireplace

Hugs or kisses?

Hugs

Do you want your friends to email you back?

Yes, poor things

When was the last time you cried?

When the IRS lady called me a liar, a cheat, a felon and a thief

What is under your bed?

Big folder of really pretty paper and bookmaking supplies

What are you afraid of?

Wolves
Penned cattle
Ostriches
jail

MRIs
Needles
Tommy Lee Jones
High freeway ramps
River snakes
US customs
The ocean
Being buried alive
My credit record
Tornadoes
Swamps
Mountains
Tunnels
The pharmaceutical military industrial complex
Scorpions in my panties

How many years at your current job?

Don't have job, am worthless

How many cities have you lived in?

One hateful little mean white town and San Antonio, and six weeks
on a hill in Vermont with black flies biting the shit out of people, and
six glorious weeks with Dylan and Luke in Chapel Hill-Carrboro
and three–four weeks in Reno which was great except for the clinic.

Sports

Ann was a sports nut, following both baseball and basketball avidly, and luckily through the heyday of the San Antonio Spurs. Ann was a proud person, and she invested her pride in her beloved teams—as her beloved writers—with ferocity, fury, and feistiness. She knew how to be a fan. Her letter to Sports Illustrated *celebrating basketball superstar David Robinson is first published here.*

—⁄⁄\~

OK, I know it don't mean a thing to more than half of you but I gotta say this in response to World Series, which I knew Rangers would lose no matter how much prayer I lifted up to heaven in their behalf.

Liza and Jackie moved to Fort Worth shortly after Dylan was born, for better financial opportunities and a better-quality life. We got used to the commutes though never the separation in distance, and enjoyed countless good times there, especially trips to Colonial Golf Course and its tournament, which was a huge deal, as well as countless absolute joys at Rangers baseball games in the old Arlington Stadium which was funky and smelled bad when it rained.

I can't come close to recalling the regularity with which we loaded up the kids and took them to Rangers games, when tickets were $5 apiece for center or right field (which we preferred) and you could bring in your own ice chest, no prob, full of your Diet Dr. Peppers, whatever the kids wanted to drink, and tons of sandwiches, and from which we could yell our adoration of Nolan Ryan, watch a nineteen-year-old Pudge Rodriguez catch his fourth game, have the rookie Juan Gonzalez touch his cap in their direction when four enthusiastic little kids shouted from way up in the stands, "Juan!" And those few years of adoring Rueben Sierra "El Indo," for whom George W.'s cat was later named. We even adored Kirby Puckett, God rest his adorable soul.

They were just never contenders but wow they were ours, in that huge mix including Fort Worth women fans for whom it was impossible to get both hair and make-up right, you would see them from behind and think this one has actually done it, her hair looks just fine, then she turned around and you saw her makeup.

One time the Rangers got on a hot streak, winning like four games in a row, and on Friday afternoon when Liza and I were speaking of our total joy about it, I just said, "We're coming"—this was when Luke was 2 or 3 in a car seat, and Dylan 9 or 10—within 30 minutes I had car loaded and left Joe a note on the kitchen stove. *We have gone to FW to see the Rangers. Look for us on the Wiener Cam.*

And we drove the seven hours in my blue convertible Mustang GT. We'd watch two games, drive back through Johnson City and Lampasas. The speed limit was 55 back then—once I got two speeding tickets within ten minutes. There was something about a Mustang convertible. I would get home at just in time to sleep a couple hours, get up and feed my three boys breakfast, load the dishwasher and be at the junior college to teach my 8 a.m.classes.

....

From a letter to *Sports Illustrated*, 1999:

You got it right, but you have to live here to know it. David Robinson has not only carried the Spurs team on his long-suffering back for the last 10 years, he and a few other Spurs have carried this whole long-suffering town. Unlike what the Daughters of the Republic of

Texas and Bob Costas would have you believe, the Alamo means about as much to the average San Antonian as any other white racist junior league–inspired social club.

You have to live in the neighborhoods, you have to work with the kids David and his teammates come to visit, talk to, inspire—the kind of kids with one pair of shoes and one Spurs t-shirt—to get it. You have to eat barbeque at Fatso's on the Fredericksburg Road to see the hope and the joy and the pride of thousands of below-blue-collar people to know that the city ain't founded on the Santa Fe de San Antonio de Padua. It's founded on the faith in the men in black, and it has been since the ABA days. It's all we got. The Baseline Bums, who have been there since the beginning, who drive old beat-up Chevys and work at gas stations and produce companies and spend probably a sixth of their annual income on tickets—we rise and fall with the Spurs.

David, Sean, Tim, Avery, Jerome, Mario, Jarren, Malik, Antonio, Steve, Will—they took us to the promised land. We saw it from the riverbank. Whether we crossed the river or not won't make any difference at all. And when you are all gone, we will know, we will remember. They defined us for 26 years fighting like we always have the almost-lost cause, but they never gave up and so we didn't, and they gave back to us more than the love we gave them, and they took us to the promised land.

Christmas

It's possible Ann was the biggest fan of Christmas there ever was. Not only the religious aspect but also the preparation and presentation of family holiday dinners was her great joy. The build-up would start weeks in advance. Have you decided on your pies? Did you start your cookies? If you didn't feel this way about the holidays, she thought there was something wrong with you.

 ⌐⁄⌐

If you pull my name from the hat in the family Christmas drawing, will you please buy me a Border Terrier puppy? I know this exceeds our limit by $1175 or $2175, but it's only money, and as you all know I don't have nearly enough dogs, especially since none of them except Bobo loves me more than Joe, and even Bobo ditches me for Neva at every opportunity.

. . . .

Everyone brought something. I had made the rolls and the Yule log and the Italian cream cake and Liza made asparagus and the world's best salad, and Gail made green beans and mashed potatoes, and once again it was fun pulling it all together, each one going to his own role. I always make the gravy, Liza always makes the table gorgeous, Papa and Lee always carve the turkeys, Luke always lights the candles and Dylan and Camille set up the card table. Mama finding us enough silver and china and crystal for all that food and drink, that banquet, and it was just the sweetest gathering ever, the sweetest blessing, and the absolutely best tasting Christmas meal ever.

Joe and I went to the ranch to feed the horses and mules. How they love their new Christmas cookies I made them. It is danger-ous—they will knock you down for more. It turned almost warm that afternoon, but by evening was very cold again, and sunset at the tank with coyotes ginning up and geese and ducks and cranes trying to land... Bucks fighting in the oat field. The startled beauty of a doe. A great horned owl.

That's how Christmas was.

....

It has been gloomy and rainy every day since Christmas but the narcissus bulbs I planted just before the holiday grew and now almost all of them are blooming, turning and bending every day toward whatever light they prefer and then straightening back up at night, smelling as sweet as hope.

Ann with her beloved mule, Chess Pie

Ann fishing in the ranch tank with her dog

Ann bottle-feeding calf

Ann with adored miniature donkeys, at home

Ann with Little Boy

Ann in the bluebonnets with her Airedale, Rummy

Ann in a field of Indian paintbrush

Ann sweet-talking a roadrunner

Joe and Naomi in family graveyard, July 2022

Ann's grave

Sunset at the ranch, with antique wagon wheels that once belonged to Ann's mother

Ann heads into the brush with her six-shooter

Marion Winik's painting of Ann on Chess Pie

Ann's boots, by Marion

The famous javelina, by Marion

no wonder Ann was terrified

The siblings, Lee, Ann, and Liza

Lee, Ann, and Liza, many years later

Ann and Joe, teenage years, at her mom's house

Joe, Ann, and baby Dylan, 1970s

Ann with Dylan and
Luke on playscape

Ann graduates from UTSA, Dylan holding diploma, Luke in arms

The family: Joe, Ann, Luke, and Dylan

Brother Lee and Ann

Ann with her granddaughters Kaitlyn and Emily (and her gun)

Ann and Joe with Emily and Kaitlyn, learning to ride

Ann with camera,
inventing the selfie,
1980s

Ann in her favorite
Texas Rangers hat

Ann with her Labradoodle, Tweed

Illness and Pain

It was a bit of a struggle in putting this book together not to let the topics of illness and pain take over. Though we all experience pain, few of us find as many ways to describe it—analyze it, rage against it, pay tribute to it, and, so importantly, laugh at it and mock it—as Ann did. In a way, it was her muse. "There was nothing ever bigger than pain, but there were little things I seized and acted upon that kept a window of light open." Writing was surely one of those things, and it was far from little. It was her life raft.

～ノ〜

I know a thousand things about pain, maybe twelve thousand. I just do know that as long as it is the main thing about your life, on any series of days longer than five, you are missing everything else, the whole rest of your life.

Oh for healing and happiness and my back not to kill me along with everything else. I hate clichés. What doesn't kill you makes you stronger. What a lie. What doesn't kill you merely doesn't kill you, and leaves you yearning to do all the things you will probably never be able to do again.

....

Every single time I sew, cook, weave, clean house, vacuum, cook or bake, sew, sing at Mass or go to my knees at Mass, transplant all the things to flower and veggie beds, gather wood with Joe, ride, fly fish or pick up children to cart here and there from pillar to post, entertain and happify them, so that every time I do what I love,

53

which I am determined to do as much as I can for the rest of my life, I'm screwed.

But I never let it stop me because I have always believed there are things "bigger than pain" and that to ride a mule, hunt and catch a fish, knead bread, lift objects as small as Corningware pans, drag babies upriver so they can float down to Papa Joe, that these are more than worth any pain they cause me, until the pain is so great that it says, "Truce over. My turn now." And that's OK. I fight for my victories, which it can punish me for but never take away because I always live for the next good time, good day, good work or good play.

....

Invalid means you are *not valid* – like an expired coupon or something. And the days go by and go by and go by. It is a spiral down and down to less and less.

....

Conversation with the doctor:
"So for me is it basically carpe diem?"
"Yes, every diem you can carp."

....

Lord, I looked better weighing 25 pounds more! I wear tunics and leggings now because nothing else fits. I am the size of an average 12-year-old boy or 2 mule feed sacks.

....

I took an internet depression test last night. Anything above a 54 was "severely depressed." My score was a 70. According to the report: "It would be advisable and likely beneficial for you to seek further diagnosis from a trained mental health professional immediately."

That part makes me laugh. I had "severe" on every symptom except for "guilt feelings" (I have very little, too little) and "loss of appetite."

....

I have new nutritional supplements from the internet to help my fibromyalgia, vitamins, snail juice for the joints, and some kind of pine bark grapeseed antioxidant, and have felt a certain overall betterness. I've been on them about three weeks, and after the first week I noticed I had some good hours almost every day. Day before yesterday, I didn't take a single painkiller until 10 pm, and that's a first for 12 years.

....

I have an unnatural love of physical comfort because I never have any. It means a great deal to me not to be wanting. . . I just want things pretty and finished and fixed and right. What the irises in the yard mean to me is that the world holds the fact of perfection, unblighted.

....

I have broken open everything fine I have been saving for years and decided that when it runs out, I will buy more. Soap and lotion and hot hot bubble baths have been a balm. . . . Honestly, I don't know how moderation ever became a virtue.

....

When my niece Camille wears her hair in a ponytail, I don't hurt as much. "Honey, put your hair in a ponytail," Liza used to say, and Camille would say, "But why?" "Because it helps Auntie's pain." "But she's not even here!" "She called and said she wanted your hair in a ponytail."

And they were 350 miles away, and this helped.

....

Pain is not a battle you win, but trench warfare, where you, on your mule, beat it back a few days. Then it regroups and mortars you.

....

I am very very tired. Chronic unmitigated pain is such a sap, it is like starting out every day beaten up. In nature I would have been devoured long ago because predators—unlike humans—can always spot the inherently damaged ones. You back yourself into a pretend life because you have no choice. No one wants to hear you scream, and so you learn not to. I had 29 years in a body I could depend on. Aside from memory loss and an inability to concentrate and losing things all the time, there is also the complete inability to understand how the rest of the world goes on its usual way while I fail and fail and fail. There is only mercy—from people who share your blood and bone, mercy in a fireplace, mercy in how the evening breezes come up, mercy in ducks in a tank, mercy in a river, mercy in oak trees and rain and the things that dazzle like a valley of bluebonnets. . .

....

Other than the tremendous blessing of the love of my family, when I turned 30 and got these horrible, pain-wracked diseases, I never had anything like a normal life. It is impossible for your life to be normal when everything has to be filtered through a tide of pain, which is often close to drowning you. At best, you tread water and still get some parts of your life accomplished.

Pain was my despot, my governor, the set of rules under which I had to carry out every job, every move, every sleeping and waking hour, every breath. My whole life had to be under its terms and according to how I could cheat it or rise larger than it or work within its hard, hard confines.

I was resigned to finding the light I could in darkness and living there as much as I could, and the balance of the dark to the light was so tipped toward the darkness. But on most days there was some good little thing, good enough for me to know I did not live in darkness all the time, and that therefore life had some degree of goodness and sweetness and meaning, that I was not just a hulking wreck of a thing. There was nothing, nothing ever bigger than pain, but there were these little things I seized and acted upon that kept a window of light open.

I have made a peace with myself about everything, about anybody's expectations of me—I know I will give each day what I can and if anyone wants to hold me to some higher standard and lay any of my failures on me—about choir practice, about schools and teachers unvisited, things unattended, obligations unmet—it will be easy for me not to care what anyone else thinks I should do, because I can only have one standard for myself, which is to give each day what I can give it.

Horrible things happen to you, and it's nobody's fault, and no, it isn't fair at all. But there it is, a fact. You can scream and hate God and hate that you have to live around your losses or you can still try to salvage a life that means something. I was blessed with the strength and will to carry on with private dignity.

....

Everything I send out is a message in a bottle. It is love, yes, and hope, but also a restorative way to spend unfathomable time. To turn the tables on pain, transmute it, transfigure it. Ship in pain; I will ship out a rug or a dog or a shawl or an Italian cream cake.

....

I was up all night in the rocking chair. Just after dawn the pain in my back and shoulders and kidneys and bladder radiated out to every part of my body, to my arms and toes and wrists and fingertips, to the follicles of my hair. It was a perfection of pain. It was holy. I understood the grace of its perfection. My mind took me to our waterfall on the river and everyone was there who had been there. I will never get to go again, but I saw its perfection, and I knew all the perfect days would lead to these hours today.

Everybody should know this dust-eating beauty of saying goodbye. The only pause button is the one you hold tight behind your eyes, holding your breath, as if by doing so you could hold forever one of the thousands of moments of joy that fell on you, or that you sweated and hurt and fought to go out and meet, and take.

P.S.

We could have had a whole book of these one-liners. Twenty thousand or so. Our favorite is the guacamole. Find yours and print the T-shirt.

⌐ʌ⌐

Oh, man, I could use a week at the river that nobody can get to anymore.

....

Why do people pray for you instead of bringing cheese and good crusty bread, grapes and olives? I think because it is easier.

....

We can send each other Kindle books for our birthdays! I just love the idea of never squirting cherry juice onto the pages.

....

My beloveds are falling like the centuries-old oak trees on the once and never again Leona River.

....

I am longing for a house where all's accustomed, ceremonious, with strawberries and Battenberg napkins.

....

I don't know how to translate what I am good at into money. The world will just never pay you very well to make dragons with third graders.

....

Happiness is work. I am glad to have learned that happiness is work.

....

You should not want to die just because you smell bat peepee in your house.

....

We name our war planes Mustang, Black Hawk, Falcon, Eagle, Phantom.

....

Don't you want to run for your life when someone comes up at a party and says he has something to share with you, and you don't see any guacamole on his plate?

....

As a human race, we just wouldn't be anywhere without sheep. We would be starving and naked.

....

The biggest things happen in the smallest places.

....

Opportunities are burdens too.

....

I won't like Heaven if it's not just like Central Texas.

....

I am plainly, insanely yours,
Ann

Weather

Ann's relationship to both heat and cold was that of a quintessential rural dweller, perpetually astonished and fascinated by its melodrama.

—⁓—

To a friend living above the Arctic Circle:

The coldest I've ever been was 3 or 4 hours at a soccer tournament in Kerrville in that stadium carved into the side of a hill, where a blue norther had blown in to clear ice blue skies and the wind was howling around us. It was about 38 degrees. I wore two pair of jeans, one lined in flannel, boots, two shirts, two wool sweaters, two Polartec jackets with a fleece-lined leather bomber jacket with the collar turned up, a Polartec cap covered by a sherpa-fur hat that came down over my ears and tied under my chin, leather gloves and three wool blankets.

And there was the soccer team out there in polyester jerseys and shorts with knee socks.

Second most miserable time was when Dylan and I decided to go out to the ranch and ride Meg and Little Boy with the temp in the windless 40s and tiny little sleet falling. We rode quietly along for several miles with that tiny sleet forming little iceballs on the horses' manes and fog coming out of their nostrils when they breathed, our eyes stinging, until finally I looked back at him and said, "Are you half as fucking cold and miserable as I am?" "Yes, but I was afraid to tell you." "Well, *I* was afraid to tell *you!*"

We bee-lined it to the pens, gave those horses extra rations of sweet feed and naturally hot alfalfa hay, warmed up his truck until the heater was running like a blast furnace, and went to the freezing, empty ranch house. We warmed our hands in hot water and over the gas stove with burners on high for fifteen minutes, but I still couldn't unbutton my fly to pee. He had to unbutton and unzip my jeans for me with pliers.

....

Every sunset, every flower or field of flowers, every cactus, every river and drought, with 117 degrees going on for days straight, it will be part of me. All the names of all the plants and trees and grasses I will know like my own. On summer evening breezes, I will smell the Gulf surf 200 miles away.

Someday I will be almost whole.

....

Del Rio got a thunderstorm and El Paso has been flooding, all we got was a damn dust storm that threw four hunnerd pounds of grit and corn shucks in the pool.

Elsewhere in Texas

As much as she may have complained about Uvalde, the rest of the state didn't quite win her over either. "I didn't hate Austin this time as much as I usually do." From Ann, this is high praise.

‑⁄⁣\‑

I believe it's a damn long way, in every possible way, from Batesville, Texas, in the fourth poorest county in the U.S.A., to Houston.

....

Part of what I love about San Antonio is that it does not hold me to the stupid social obligations my hometown holds women to. You are always obligated to be at some damned wedding shower. . .

....

The drive home from Austin on the freeway was harrowing. They have a whole bunch of it crunched together into two tiny lanes with concrete fences about four feet high on both sides and the speed limit is supposed to be 45 but people go 70 and all the way here there was so much traffic. . . I couldn't understand why so many people had to be somewhere on a Sunday afternoon. . . I think [I-]35 to Austin from San Antonio is the meanest and most dangerous freeway on earth.

I didn't hate Austin this time as much as I usually do. People were incredibly white-trash and nice. I didn't notice anybody putting on any People for the Ethical Treatment of Animals airs, and nobody coughed outdoors in the dire face of my secondhand smoke.

....

**Upon moving to San Antonio to study
for a master's in English:**

Knowing in me that I must subject myself to things which are not
"safe" and "secure," knowing that I must not atrophy, must always
strive, must test myself, must never become soft, must grow, must
learn, must accomplish, must face a terrifying world, the unknown;
must not allow myself to become solidified in a content world, must
never be too contented, must always have the tension that challenges
the mind, must conquer the fears that terrify the soul . . . I've come
to San Antonio to school.

Terrifying accomplishments: traffic, finding my way to the school,
getting lost, finding the right buildings, registration, finding bath-
rooms, answering questions, FIND THE BUS STOPS, GETTING
OFF AT THE RIGHT PLACE . . . pressures of reading, responding,
discussing (so lost, insignificant), preparing and delivering an oral
report in the midst of the competitiveness, hands shaking, voice
breaking. . .

The oral presentation went well. We had been talking about "opium
for the masses" in a Hemingway story and I began my talk by say-
ing, "I wish I had some opium" which was true and which pleased
my audience.

Love

Here Ann's precise attention and deep emotional responsiveness to the world around her are crystallized as pure celebration. What she is so inspired by in "the foodies" parallels her own appetite for life. For them, it's a potato, for her, of course, it's a mule.

— ⁊ ⦅ ⸍

I am in love with a thousand things. Friends from kindergarten and their children. My brother and sister and their kids and my father and husband and my six dogs (really I only love four of them), thousands of students I have taught over the years. l have been in love with two horses and am currently in love with a mule. I am in love with fires in the fireplace, the Nueces River which has been privatized and taken from me even though it formed me more than any single thing other than being raised a Catholic and learning to ride horses just at the time most kids learn to be shits.

I am in love with horned toads and javelinas and the beautiful work of gun dogs. I am in love with the smell of whitebrush at the end of the day when the hot hot air is first cooling into a breeze, I love and want every breed of terrier I ever saw except for the Manchesters, Skyes, Silkies, and Scotties. I am in love with fuji apples and gala apples and fresh cherries. I am in love with God and Jesus and Mary and St. Anthony whom I treat in heaven as my love slave—people call me from thousands of miles away to ask for his intercession so that they may find something.

I am so in love with my granddaughters that I spend hours imagining what they are doing and what we would be doing if we were together. I am in love with the smell of rain on dirt, which fortunately my Border Terrier pup smells exactly like even when it's not raining which for the last 7 years it never has. I am in love with every fish I catch on my fly rod whether large or smaller than my hand, each one gives me equal pleasure, I unhook them and kiss them and thank them for the joy they gave me before I release them back into the rare silvery green ribbons of water which flow through our county. l also love bread and every kind of real cheese except for the Stiltons and bleus and limburgers.

I am in love with movies and books, history books and biographies and Harry Potter and *The Jungle Books* Volume I and II and *The Adventures of Huckleberry Finn*. *The Tempest* and the Tennyson poem "Ulysses" and too many written things to write. I am in love with several poems without which I do not consider that the life of a soul can be complete, with "The Bear" by William Faulkner and with every sentence Hemingway ever wrote.

I am in love with oak trees and dry creek beds and great horned owls and all the little birds and big ones that come to the 15 bird feeders around our house, especially the green jays who are supposed to migrate but haven't in four years, the cardinals, the fleeting rare painted buntings and the greater and lesser goldfinches that eat from the thistle sacks outside the window upside down, like Dracula. I love the little palomas tristes, the tiny fat mourning doves, and I love but not as much their older cousins the whitewing doves who crash into feeders spilling half the food from each.

I am in love with Texas Horned Lizards which everyone calls horny toads, and praying mantises, all sunfish and perch, and largemouth bass. I can't decide whether little baby goats, little baby pigs, or little baby calves are cuter but I can testify that little newborn pink javelinas are the cutest animals in creation.

l love my house, I love to weave and sew, I love sunflowers, zinnias, Mexican birds of paradise, esperanza and red crape myrtle though all of mine is hot pink. I love to garden and for holidays I love to cook, especially exotic deserts and homemade sourdough bread or rolls and fancy piped gingerbread and shortbread cookies and popcorn balls that burn my hands.

....

Have you ever noticed that the stories people tell you about their own lives, or the lives of other people you love, are rarely something you were witness to? You're never with people when the good stories are actually happening.

Then you take what they told you freely about their lives and you write that down and feel like you have, by trying to get to the essence of those you love, invaded their privacy. It is sort of like being in your mother's bathroom when you are little, or opening the drawers where she kept her silky things, and little velvet pockets with pearls in them. Things that smelled like your mother. Sort of like going upstairs in somebody's house. Upstairs is intimate. And what people do at night. It's like a curtain opening, unbearably sweet and vulnerable. How separate almost everybody you love is from you at night. How each one or each group goes off into something that will never include you.

I have never been Liza's neighbor, to see her Christmas tree at night.

....

On foodies:

I am not a foodie but I love foodies. I love watching the joy they take from watching the food channel and reading recipe magazines or books and how their heroes [are] Paula Dean or the Nealys or Julia Child or Emeril. I love how much the idea of good food pleases them, gives them something gorgeous to look forward to, how they improvise it, invent it, place some of the finest meals I've ever eaten on a plate in front of me, and together we sat and savored every bite and every ingredient. I love the tender care they take with their food, like the way I carefully groom and saddle and bridle a horse or mule.

I love how they already know the very best dish on the menu of every restaurant so I don't make the mistake of ordering a burger. I love how they know the best restaurants on every budget. I love how they dwell on food as they drive home from work, thinking of the concoctions they are going to amalgamate into something divine for supper. I love how they talk to each other about a recipe, about what little touch (store-bought breadcrumbs in addition to days-old homemade bread) makes one bread pudding or capirotada a thousand times better than the next one.

I love how foodies substitute when they're out of something a recipe calls for. I love how they post on Facebook how delicious the home-made chicken pot pie was and where they went to eat for supper and how damned good it was. I love perusing the recipes they've collected since the time of their grandmother's friends, and how this or that is scratched through with a different amount or ingredient substituted. I love to watch them hold a glass of beautiful yellow wine in one hand and a meat cleaver in the other, talking to me about anything at all, at the same time fiddling with kids and pets and the dishwasher. I love their high-quality, glistening pots and pans, beaters and meat-whackers and whisks and wooden spoons and potato mashers and tiny, tiny little sieves and graters. I love that they know 7,386 things to do with a potato or an egg or a batch of asparagus.

I can't love food like that. I love my mule like that.

....

To a bereaved friend:

God blessed me with six gorgeous pink peonies the size of home-coming mums from my four-year-old peony plant this spring. This is not supposed to be possible south of the line of Mason and Dixon. Yet I took full credit for it with everyone I told. Only you will understand each of them to your father's soul, and to your waves of grief.

Lee

Ann's outsized passion for her brother Lee pole-vaulted him to heroic status. Losing him was a devastating blow that inspired a vast outpouring of writing over many years.

✧

I remember how beautiful Lee was walking, no matter where. He had this long-strided, not too fast stroll, in any place, and like any outdoorsman his eyes were casting about. From the brush around him and for arrowheads and to the far horizon. It was the same whether he was in new country or his own. He was taking in beauty with every step, and never talked. With our long backs and my long stride I matched him print for print.

Sometimes he would stop and look far away and say, Look at that buck on the edge of the hill. It would be so far away. He walked so easily on this earth, covered ground not rapidly but not slowly. Papa always stopped to pick up something up close but not Lee.

Lee was always about what was around the next bend. He walked very lightly for a man so tall. I would hear his quiet breaths. His ease in his own skin. There is the whole of him and then there are the parts of him that come to me a bit at a time. The way he held his hat, the way he held his reins. I am so grateful to remember it.

Liza walks with a lope, Joe walks with quick purpose, Lee walked as if there were an unknown purpose in each easy step. He walked real slow around the mules and horses and spoke so softly. "Hello darlin." I remember him with a cat in his lap. . . . I remember how he stood with his hands on his hips in the horse pen just waiting for them to come to him. I remember his long slow easy breaths. It is all so gorgeous.

I remember how he held an infant in one arm like a loaf of bread. For hours and hours on end. How he never despaired of all-night endless colic. How furious he got at cattle and machinery, how he walked the rows of his crops, sniffing or biting them, how he held his temper with small animals (not cattle in pens who needed castrating, deworming, immunization) and people.

I remember how he would lift the soil into both hands, grind it, smell it and toss it away. I remember him with an orphan calf or my sick huge Airedale slung over his saddle. I remember how he chewed on a grain of tall brown grass, how when we were riding he would pluck off a ripe persimmon and eat it. I remember saying, Let's ride to that pincushion cactus and he led me across all the acres to the very one I meant.

I remember how he loved baby goats and always smelled them and wrapped them in his jacket if they were cast off. I remember how in a fluid motion he led the shotgun before the sporting clays and hit doubles. I remember him always stooping to pick up his shells. I remember how gently he unhooked a bass, admired and freed it. I remember him walking among the javelina families to give them more corn. I remember how he knew all the planets, the winter and summer constellations and where they would be.

I remember how he loved Christmas and the shirt he always wore Christmas Eve, and how gifts always made him cry. I remember how he knew the Spanish and English names for all the plants, cacti, and trees. Some of the names were Aztec. I remember how for no reason he would give one of my sons a knife or a gun. I remember how when he was reading he always pulled on his eyebrows. I remember how thin his voice was when diabetes was eating him organ by organ.

I remember in halftime of an NFC conference final football game, Kaitlyn took him by the hand and said, "Come on Lee. Let's go riding," and how immediately he got up from the game and obeyed.

I remember how I would come home from work and the kitchen table would be full of lettuce or corn or cantaloupes or cabbages. A doctor told him his heart was going to blow up, soon, and how he never told us. Now when I think of him looking into the distance from the porch, I think it was a farther distance than any of us knew. I remember every ritual of evening, the hug and "Goodbye, darlin, I'll see you later on in the week."

....

There were sycamore leaves everywhere. Lee had a piece of straw or grass in his mouth. Liza's dress was that beautiful old-fashioned light orange with a little print on it.

I had on a navy or midnight blue velveteen jumper with matching hat and a little puff sleeve white cotton blouse with Peter Pan collar. Lee's shirt was pale green stripe with white and one thread of silver separating them. Look at how sweetly Liza has her arm around me. I was four, Liza seven, Lee ten. Time did not weigh on us. We were adored.

I was already magic and still assumed that everybody was. One day would lead to another, which would lead to another, forever.

You never have the sense that death will separate you, not from your sister and brother. What brings back life when a third of you is gone?

....

Here is a scar I earned all by myself and yet, like with all of them, you are its cause. My being brave enough to follow you, even where I cannot go.

....

Sometimes Chess Pie looks at me asking, Where is that other one who loved me? Their memories are as long as elephants' and I see her looking for him. The tack barn emptied of his saddle and the blanket I wove him which made him cry feels like a hole you could fall into the bottom of the earth from. I received two visits from him and know I will never receive another. Four nights after he died he waked me up with his full strong well voice and said, "Aww hell Ann, it's only death."

And two months ago I was looking out the kitchen window at the bird feeder, and in the distance Lee in his khakis and chaps and long-sleeve shirt and narrow-brimmed felt hat riding Leona, turned back to look at me, to be sure I was still safe and there, like he had done a thousand times in our lives, and his gaze stayed smiling fixed on me before he turned his head and disappeared into the brush. I know it was goodbye. He was telling me he was all right and that I would be too, and that like always, one day I would follow. He was telling me to say goodbye and be at peace, which I was for a month.

Family

Anyone who has spent time with Ann and her family falls in love with her husband Joe. He is a quiet presence in life as he also is in her writing. All her family members, living and dead, became characters on the page—most of them far more private than Ann and less inclined to acknowledge conflicts and troubles. Her prayer at the end of this section, to be worthy of her loved ones, is an endearing plea for forgiveness. She knew she was not an easy person.

━╱╲━

Liza Dreams the Irises

Nancy brings me, in a white vase,
An iris, the color of her eyes.
Liza dreams the iris bulbs
I gave her in a poem last fall
Bloomed profusely in her yard, and
plucking away the withered ones, she
discovered growing underneath
Birds of paradise.

. . . .

Hello darlings, Please don't find this morbid. This is all but the picture taken of us gathered after the sweet burial of Mama's ashes in a darling black cast iron Dutch oven Papa had bought her long ago at Horner's.

Joe's way of healing and getting through the days was to spend untold hours at our family cemetery clearing brush and dragging up wonderful old tree logs and building precious rustic benches out of railroad ties. Weeks ahead of time he spread bird seed and corn all along the ground so that each evening as he sat at the graveyard, he was gradually surrounded by dozens and dozens of green jays, redbirds, raccoons, turkeys, possums, javelina, and WAY too many feral hogs for my comfort. I texted him, Joe, I would much prefer that you not become so familiar with the damned hogs, I just lost my mother and I need not to find my husband half-chewed up by feral hogs and bury you too!

He set old, weathered pieces of wood in cement to make a cross for her, and the night before Thanksgiving he went out to dig the circular grave. Everything was exactly as she would have had it. There is something really holy and intimate and sweet which the funeral industry removes you from, but it is healing and wholesome and necessary to take turns picking up that shovel one by one and filling in Mama's grave, and after we all had our turn Joe and Lee kindly finished the job as a huge angus cow lumbered up from the riverbed and made her way to wherever she intended to go.

The tenderest thing for me was that sweet Papa wanted to be left alone there for thirty minutes while the rest of us raced off to get veggies in and out of ovens, wine popped, gravy made. I know he partly stayed because in all these years he had never seen a green jay and knew they now gathered there, and also just to be with the last of Mama.

Green jays are rare, well, until this year it was rare to see them, except along the riverbed at the ranch during their winter migration from Mexico. Now I hear their darling self-important caws every morning, since they know they are the boss of everyone and can run off as many cardinals as they want. I wouldn't be a bit surprised if the western bluebirds came back in the late-late-winter/early spring, for only the second time ever. This may sound strange, but God has always marked the big occasions of my life with rare birds or the exact right bird at the right time, the way a gorgeous green hummingbird showed up in the empty tree branches outside the church after precious hummingbird heart Aunt Biddy's funeral.

On the way to Mama's burial, a white heron crossed the Batesville Road, right above our car. Grey and blue herons, yes, all the time, but a white heron? Breathtaking for these parts. On the day we chose her gravesite, my favorite bird the great horned owl flew in a whoosh of powerful wings above the trail to the car. Joe said, "Ann, that was your great horned owl," and I said, "Yeah, what else would it be."

In certain moods, great white herons get this hilarious white punky coxcomb that reminds you of those whimsical hats English women wear to Ascot. Mama always loved it when beauty added ridiculousness to itself with no apology or dread of tackiness, like when Raphael added one or two more precious putti to a painting than taste and decorum required. I reckon everyone who knows me can understand that my religion is enhanced and not defiled by birds, donkeys, dogs, whitebrush blooming, Dutch irises and sunflowers, the Nueces River, the Grand Canyon, and fly-fishing, whether this makes me semi-pagan or no.

....

It was beautiful tonight to be sitting with dearest loved ones at the Wagnons' fire pit on their deck, to look across the riverbed and up the little hill a bit and see all the twinkling white lights around the ranch house where I knew Liza and Papa were finishing their martinis and having supper and reading, less than a mile away from us. I was thinking to myself, The lights are still on and my Papa is still here, where he most loves to be.

....

From her eulogy for her father:

Papa was sort of an Ernest Hemingway without all the wives. In the deep seas he caught champion marlin, sailfish, and tarpons, and in the shallows he and Mama caught bonefish. With Lee in South American jungle rivers, he loved to catch the beautiful fighting peacock bass. In the mountains he climbed in Alaska after long training in his 50s (he refused to be helicoptered in, considering that unsporting), he took a Dahl Sheep, a mountain goat, a moose, and a caribou, which the hunting party ate. He considered it unsporting to kill a bear or elephant or leopard or anything inedible, or any of the non-sporting critters that live here on this ranch. Deer, game birds in season, and as many feral hogs as you could get were fine. But he wanted the javelinas, cougars, badgers, coyotes, and bobcats left alone to live their lives here in peace. He recently told Joe that all the time he had spent hunting, if he could do it over again, he would have spent it fishing.

....

A pilgrimage:

All of us cousins, or as many as possible from all over the country went to Menard right after Thanksgiving 2009 in a kind of pilgrimage to retrace our Callan/Waring family roots and to FINALLY place a tombstone on the grave site of little Michael John Callan who lived 4 days, Mama's and all of their infant brother.

As it turned out, the tombstone I picked had little cornflowers on it which reminded me of my saddle leather, and when we looked at Grandma's brother's tombstone, Harold "Doc" Waring the world's greatest cowboy whose saddle I inherited at age 12 and have ridden ever since, that tombstone had the EXACT SAME DESIGN as his little tiny nephew's.

At the time of their baby's death, back in the 30s, Grandma and Grandpa were too poor and broke and broken to give their baby a tombstone, so we fixed that 60 years later and it made Mama so happy to know we had all done that.

....

I hated swimming lessons. I didn't want that smiling twenty-year-old man to lift me off the pool edge with fifteen kids lined up watching, and I told Mama I was never going back. Mama was so good at understanding never. Two weeks later, Liza taught me to swim in the Leona River.

....

I am convinced that women are charged with 99% of the graciousness necessary to tend to the things that give life its beauty and continuity. Tomorrow, Liza and I meet to do another thing that always fall on women. Like picking flowers for the church. And who will write which thank-you notes. We will divide up all the kind things that must be done.

Men carry away the garbage, and return the borrowed tables and chairs, and dig the holes, and it is over.

....

I have spent the afternoon full of almost-tearful nostalgia. I ordered 2 CDs of classic western songs from movies, TV shows & radio— Gene Autry, Roy Rogers, Sons of the Pioneers, Paladin, Bonanza, Rawhide, Cheyenne, Johnny Cash, Tex Ritter, Marty Robbins—and I just had this profound longing for those days that seemed to me innocent—of course they weren't—they had racism, hatred, oppression—but I just wanted everybody back.

....

To her mama:

I think maybe the mystical part of me makes you a little bit nervous, like Beulah Barber's spirit writing. Did you know it happens to me all the time now at the ranch? Almost every time I am by myself with Chess Pie and the dogs, natural as breathing? I didn't tell you but when I was sitting by what is left of the poor old white tank and Chess Pie bent her head down to be near mine, Grandma and Grandpa and Jimmy were right there, too. Not apparitions but just presences. And God they loved me! And I loved them back.

I remember thinking, I want to go with them, and realizing I already am.

....

On racism:

I go to the mat every single time. I have actually been chastised for this.
"Why do you have to say that, it made us so uncomfortable?"
I say, "No, the person who said the racist words made us all uncomfortable."
"You should just let it go."
"Your child isn't half Mexican."
"You need to get the chip off your shoulder."
"Walk in Joe's shoes for a day or a week."

....

We must vow never to do anything with our extra money but travel. And I don't mean to Italy or Paree, but even to little cross-eyed towns in the Ozarks. I want to take the kids to mini golf. In Batesville, Arkansas.

....

I have a propensity to panic attacks at weddings and funerals during that time when you are all squashed in waiting for them to start. I had to leave JC's funeral and at Derek's I nearly died.

....

Lord, make me a source of love and joy to everyone who loves me, stop me from being spoiled, make me lovable so I am good for people, so I have some company on this switchback, so that the ones I drove off, I will see how I did it and make amends and not be alone through all the long days and longer nights, show me where I need to ask forgiveness, please bring them back not as a visit of charity but as a force that makes them happy, and every day show me how I can do better and be better for the dear ones I love, bring them back to me, make me worthy of being brought back to, and forgive me for ending an independent clause of a compound sentence with a preposition.

Motherhood

Ann saw herself as a proudly unconventional mom, but her dreams about who she would be as a grandmother are exquisitely universal.

—⁊⫯⹁—

I was the most relaxed carefree careless easygoing mother of children in the world. I nearly let them drown in the riptides of the Atlantic Ocean as l dozed on the beach and brushed away ghost crabs. I let them follow the water-moccasin-and-dope-smoker-filled Leona River all the way back to the dam at Mt. Inge from the time they were seven. When they fell off horses crying, I told them to get up and get back on. I have sat through five emergency room visits without ever shedding a tear. I bicycled with them down freeways in North Carolina when they were 11 and 5.

I let them drive standard cars all over the ranch when they only knew automatic. I entrusted them with guns at the age of l3 to kill doves and rattlesnakes and the coons or skunks invading the chicken coop. I lied for them cavalierly to school attendance clerks & and wrote sincere excuses for them when they skipped school to go to the Nueces River, which you know to be a fine and essential thing for any group of high school kids to do. l never objected when their father bought their necessary beer, snuff, etc. from age 16 on. I have not heard from Son #1 for months at a time, when he was a free-range chicken, working here and there on the road, and I never worried about his safety, or assumed that anything was wrong with him, or that I had failed him as a mother.

. . . .

The first surrender is when we see them newborn from our bodies, when they break our hearts and we realize it is part of the deal, that every mother's child will break her heart over and over again. Motherhood is just too big for the heart, to have an unbroken heart would be unnatural. Your heart wouldn't even feel like its own self if it weren't breaking... but by now you know it doesn't really break, it just stretches wider and wider.

....

Of her grandchild:

I want to be her ace in the hole. I want her to dig up doodlebugs and worms and know how other people's memories suddenly imprint on our brains. I want her to believe in what cannot be seen. I want some poem or painting or piece of music or treehouse to mean more than anything to her, I want her to have primal totems, like Walden Pond. I want her to find her own and not just go to the mall, and make good grades, and progress well in phonics. I want her to fall into books and myths and landscapes. I want to be her secret weapon.

Grief

Even at the age of twenty-four Ann was acutely aware of all that we stand to lose in our lives. The last piece of writing in this section is the earliest-written piece in this book, yet it seems to contain the guiding spirit that controlled the whole rest of her life.

‑⁄⁋‑

Written five months after her mother's death:

I decided I would give myself a year to be whatever each day brought to me and how little I brought to it, to fulfill or not fulfill my obligations, to cry until I cried less, to sit until I decided to stand, not to want until I wanted something. To be crazy if I were, and unreliable and unresponsive and tardy or absent. That I would give myself a year to just let my life happen to me. Then after a year I would go out and eat my life again.

But for a year I could be as unreliable as the stopped rain if I needed to, and everybody had to forgive me for everything as I silently asked for their mercy. I believed their mercy toward my absence and irresponsibility would be a kind of grace to befall them. They said, "But she wouldn't WANT you to be like this, she would want you to wake up and want to live!" I thought, "She would be exactly as I am."

The rest of my family took up their lives again bravely and dutifully and valiantly. They stood up and did what must be done each day. I am the laggard. The raw harshest depth of grief abated after five months enough for me to make some small effort on some days to begin to take my life back. I pray more now, I read the texts and readings for each day's Mass. I keep up with loved ones and friends with email and texts. But if anyone were to ask me what I do with my life I would say, "Birds. I watch the beautiful birds at all the feeders I can see from my chair."

I watch the darling hummingbirds fight for territory at the feeder, I watch the whitewing doves crash into the feeders spilling half the feed, I watch the gorgeous cardinals and tiny black tits, and the Bullocks oriole couple who have built a woven hanging nest high in the dead fronds of one of our palm trees, come in to drink from the hummingbird feeder. I watch for rare daily glimpses of the gorgeous painted bunting and the majestic green jays who stayed. My greatest pleasure is the four socks of tiny black thistle seed on which 7 to 15 goldfinches and house finches are all eating all the time, half of them upside down, little vampires. The goldfinches are so tiny that when they light on leaves, the leaves don't even dip down; they must weigh two ounces.

Watching them, loving them, is an act of solidarity with my life, what it was, what it must become in some lessened but still life-eating way, the way we hunger for our lives to be full and leave pieces of the beauty we saw or made and were grateful for, for somebody, for our children or theirs, the way we want to count and have meaning and leave a record of gratitude and make our grandchildren laugh or hold something reverently in their hands in years to come, "This my grandmother made." "This my grandmother wrote."

My beloved friend Naomi once wisely wrote me at a strange and sad crossroads in my life, "We can never know what happens next." I think we can never know what brings us back. I am not back, I am far from back, but my journey has begun taking me somewhere, in arduous steps that sometimes go forward or sideways or tripping me into scab-kneed falls. It goes somewhere I can never know where next. For me, the steps back toward life are watching the birds gorging themselves on food they love. Hour by hour goes to day by day, and ounce by ounce for me.

....

I already feel Andrew Marvell's TIME hovering over me, and so much in me wants to say *stop, I get off here.* . . so much I have put off, saying later, when this is done, or as soon as I finish this, I'll tend to it. . . I never grasp Mr. B's old, calloused hand to leave him that I do not think, *I may never see him again.* He taught me how to ride and how to live. I never slide off Blondie's slick back that I do not think, *Someday she will not be* (imagine—I was 12 and now I am 24—half my life that gentle nature always there, always ready to come to me). All is loss, just like Wordsworth said. The only control we have over time is how we use it.

Afterword

Marion Winik

When Naomi and I started going through Ann's writing in 2018, and a few years later, as I drafted the first version of our book proposal, I had a certain way to explain the project to people. I would describe the decades of correspondence, the mountains of letters and emails and Facebook posts Ann produced in her life. I would say that I thought of her as an "outsider writer," sort of like the outsider artists in Baltimore's American Visionary Art Museum.

I would explain that though she rarely worked on official manuscripts or sought publication—her illness made submission seem a burden—she loved the idea of us doing the work for her. The book became a treasured idea that came up frequently in our correspondence. But then there was the little dust-up about Naomi's brainstorm for the cover art that led her to suggest we publish posthumously.

I always concluded with the fact that she was a profoundly Texas-y writer, from a little place in South Texas you never heard of.

That last bit changed on Tuesday, May 24, 2022, when Uvalde became a place everyone has heard of, the same way they've heard of Columbine, Sandy Hook, Parkland, and Aurora. As the news came in, even before we knew that Ann's ten-year-old great-niece Layla Salazar was among the lost, it crossed both of our minds that it was a blessing Ann didn't live to see this. How could she have borne it? On the other hand, she would have had so much to say about it. Interestingly, as we continued sifting through the material in the months after the shooting, it seemed she already had said some of these things.

Her writing about grief and loss, about civility as a response to discord, her struggle with faith in the face of terrible pain: all seemed to have a new resonance. At the same time, it was as if the true original nature of Uvalde, the little place in South Texas hardly anybody ever heard of, with its feral pigs and green jays and mules and families celebrating Christmas, was preserved in amber by her writings about it.

We had always planned for me to come down so we could visit Uvalde together and meet with Ann's husband Joe. I wanted to see the places that were important to her, particularly the ranch that was at the center of her life since childhood. I had a plane ticket to fly down in the summer of 2022, and then the school-shooting tragedy occurred in May. We wondered: *Should we still go?* The answer was yes, of course. It was more important than ever, really.

Luckily we arrived in Uvalde after the hordes of media and other doom-related visitors had departed. The town had returned to what I imagined was its normal level of traffic and commotion (mostly wind and birdsong.) Yet the sorrow was everywhere you looked, from the Welcome to Uvalde sign on the edge of town, to the grounds of the elementary school, to the town square, all marked with crosses, heaped with stuffed animals and withered bouquets, posted with scrawled notes and printed signs of support from police and fire departments and school districts all over Texas and beyond. Downtown there were stencils of angels in the shop windows alongside the brand-new Children's Bereavement Center. The old-fashioned ice cream parlor and gaily colored candy store whispered the names of their missing patrons. Even the sign for a flooring distributor called Fresh Start Decoration seemed aware of the discouraging odds against fresh starts.

Around many corners of downtown, in hidden alleys, overlooking empty lots, muralists from all over the state were painting the beautiful shining faces of the twenty-one victims. Near our Airbnb, a sparkling, whitewashed refuge in the oldest building in town, an artist on a scaffold and her assistant worked through the night.

Locals were surprised and then pleased that we had actually shown up to talk about something else. Something else! We started with Mendell Morgan, the eighty-one-year-old city librarian whom Naomi had first met when she came to put on the first in series of healing workshops with artists and writers at the library. We joined Mendell for lunch at a place called Oasis Outback. Like a truck stop, Oasis Outback had a huge gift shop that led into multiple capacious paneled dining rooms. All were festooned with the heads of thirty-point bucks, bobcats, and other taxidermic critters. The tables were full of what looked like the entire population of Uvalde and the surrounding region. It seemed to be the official cafeteria of the town, frequented by law enforcement, large families, and ladies who lunch. Its soup and salad bar was the living image of "Texas-sized" and featured the most generous definition of salad imaginable, which included numerous desserts. Mendell, however, forswore these postprandial options and ordered all three of us cups of the soft-serve chocolate-and-vanilla-swirl ice milk, which had the magical quality of seeming to come from all three of our very different childhoods. Naomi and I insisted we would split a cup and then found our spoons dueling over the last bite.

We fell so in love with Mendell, who moved back from San Antonio to his hometown after his wife's death twelve years earlier, that we also had dinner with him that night and breakfast the next day. He took us to a palatial and brilliantly air-conditioned bank where former governor Dolph Briscoe's art collection was hung for public viewing. Chandeliers dangled over upholstered red leather club chairs and rockers, welcoming the weary public. Along the way, we dreamed up ever more elaborate events and parties to have upon the publication of Ann's book, which we thought might come out around the one-year anniversary of the tragedy, offering that soft promise of something else, something more.

In the gift shops along Main Street we met Ann's old neighbors, the daughter of one of her classmates—we met no one who didn't know who she was. But every time Naomi and I introduced ourselves and explained our project, I had to add that actually I had never met her. Even Naomi was surprised by this. But it's a fact. I never did. Naomi started forwarding Ann's letters to me in the late nineties, and cc'ing her on my responses, which led to her including me on her to-lists and eventually anointing me as one of the editors of her hopefully posthumous book. I am pretty sure we never even spoke on the phone. But here I am.

The surprisingly youthful and good-humored Joe Alejandro, Ann's husband of forty-five years, arrived in his truck to take us out to the ranch, where we planned to meet with Ann's son Dylan and his wife Jennifer. Joe is a sturdy, handsome man who still has a full head of hair in his seventies. He had brought all their old photo albums for us to look at and was happy to tell all the stories we wanted to hear. How they met in high school, at eighteen and seventeen, and married a year later, the interracial alliance so upsetting that some of Ann's aunts wrote her father Herbie begging him to put his foot down. Joe talked a lot about his father-in-law Herbie Toombs—the men were clearly close, allied by their interests in farming, home improvement, and golf. Later that night, out for a drink with our librarian friend, Joe would teach me to order a gin and tonic Herbie Toombs–style—a double shot of Bombay Sapphire in a short glass. On some subjects, I can be a fast learner.

The dirt road leading into the ranch through acres of scrubland seemed very long, more than the three miles Joe said it was. But as soon as we passed through the gate, we were greeted by a mama cow and her calf. *You came to see animals?* they seemed to say. *Well, here we are.* Nearby, a number of longhorn bulls grazed, surveying their patrimony, not straying too far from the water tank, which is probably all that's keeping them and the deer, the ocelots and the coyotes, the ducks and the geese, and even the jackrabbits going in the drought that has been going on for years now. Twelve years, by some counts I find online.

We went up to the little graveyard I knew well from Ann's writing, where the green jays sang at her mama's funeral, where Ann herself is now buried alongside her beloved brother Lee and her parents and grandparents. Joe sat in the rusty swing, his head bowed. After a while, he told us that he plans to dig his own hole next to Ann. "So my boys won't have to do it," he said. But that time seemed a long way off. After another while, Joe's phone buzzed with a message from Dylan, the older of his and Ann's sons, telling him to bring us on up to the house.

Though we were told the house in question was carted onto the land in flatbed trucks after the original house, built on the highest spot on the property, burned down during a wild lightning storm on Sunday, May 28, 2017, it looked completely natural in its wooded setting. Past the large wooden deck, a sprinkler waved prisms of water beneath the lowest branches of the loblolly pines. "What are you watering?" I asked Jennifer.

"The dirt," she said. "To keep it on the ground." Then she took me in the house to introduce me to her nine cats and pour me a glass of deliciously cold red wine. She showed me a picture of her daughter Kaitlyn at her high school graduation earlier this year. She is holding a certificate that declares her the winner of the Ann Toombs Alejandro scholarship for creative writing, which she is now putting to good use at one of the branches of Texas A&M. Another writer in the family. Granny Annie, as they called her, would love that.

In the hour we spent on the porch with Dylan, Jennifer, and Joe, I understood for the first time that not only Layla Salazar but also the boy who murdered her and her classmates and teachers is a blood relation of this extended family. The hurt is too much to hold. It curdles to anger, roils and rages inside Dylan. The sense that this place, his place, his home, has been irredeemably altered, and that he couldn't stop it and no one else stopped it, is almost unbearable. Here on the ranch, even, the violation makes itself felt.

Dylan and his father feel very strongly about guns: they can't imagine a life without them. Naomi and I know this. We know that Joe has a gun in the truck right now. When we were editing Ann's letters, we read pages and pages of proud pro-gun sentiment, some of it specifically in reaction to the Columbine shooting. In my younger years, I likely would have felt compelled to bring this up with the Alejandro men. In my seventh decade, I have the sense to just listen.

Then suddenly, it was 8:23 p.m. "You better go, or you'll miss it," Dylan said. He knew I was hoping to see a ranch sunset, something Ann had written about many times. We offered quick goodbyes and thanks and promises to return, then ran to the truck, and Joe somehow got us to the top of the hill where the main house used to be in negative-two minutes, just in time. The original stone fireplace still stood, alongside two small rooms Joe put up and lived in for a while. There were several rusty barbecue smokers. And there was the big Texas sky, ribboned with peach as the burning ball disappeared at the close of the day.

As Ann put it, and to give her the last word:

Chess Pie and I go to a world without words; at sunset there is a rounding road on a hill from which we can see not a sign of any human at all, only the bowl of sky equaled to the earth around us. We can see southwest to the clouds forming on the Gulf of Mexico that will bring us the wind in the evening; we look north and we can see the Uvalde water towers, Mount Inge, the hills at Knippa, and the hills of all three rivers which spill into the valleys—the Nueces, the Frio, and the Sabinal.

Every sunset, every flower or field of flowers, every cactus, every river and drought, with 117 degrees going on for days straight, it will be part of me. All the names of all the plants and trees and grasses I will know like my own. On summer evening breezes, I will smell the Gulf surf 200 miles away.

Someday I will be almost whole.

Acknowledgments

Naomi and Marion would like to thank

Joe, Dylan, and Jennifer Alejandro
Steve Davis
Chris Dodge
Ted and Katy Flato
Thom Lemmons
Mendell Morgan
Michael Nye
Liza Toombs

Ann requested that donations in her memory be made to any orangutan, elephant, or black rhino sanctuary or foundation, or to any rescue organization for homeless pets. Now we imagine she might also suggest Uvalde's El Progreso Memorial Library, to help the kids of the town she loved so much enjoy more special events, more comforting books, and more celebrations of the joy that telling one's own story can bring.

About the Editors

NAOMI SHIHAB NYE (opposite page, right) received the Lon Tinkle Lifetime Achievement Award from the Texas Institute of Letters and the Ivan Sandrof Lifetime Achievement Award from the National Books Critics Circle. She has been Young People's Poet Laureate of the United States (Poetry Foundation), poetry editor for the *New York Times Magazine*, and poetry editor for the *Texas Observer*. She has written or edited more than thirty books, including *Grace Notes* and *The Tiny Journalist*. She has worked as a visiting writer all her life, currently at Texas State University and was proud to call Ann Alejandro friend for nearly four decades.

MARION WINIK (opposite page, left) is the author of *The Big Book of the Dead*, *First Comes Love*, *Above Us Only Sky*, and other books. She reviews books for *People*, the *Washington Post*, *Oprah Daily*, and others, and hosts *The Weekly Reader* podcast on National Public Radio. She teaches in the MFA program at the University of Baltimore. She and Naomi met in 1980 at a writers' conference in Austin. More information available at marionwinik.com.